GRANDMOTHER EARTH VI: 2000

Patricia Smith
Frances Brinkley Cowden
Editors

Featuring
Award-winning
Poetry and Prose
from the
1999 GRANDMOTHER EARTH
NATIONAL WRITING CONTEST

Featuring
Alabama Poets and Writers and
Winners of the Inez Elliot Anderson Award

GRANDMOTHER EARTH CREATIONS
Memphis, Tennessee

Copyright ©2000 by Grandmother Earth Creations
ALL RIGHTS RESERVED
Individual works belong to the individual authors. This book or parts thereof may not be reproduced without permission from the individual authors or publisher except for customary privileges extended to the press and other reviewing agencies.
Work previously published was used by permission of the individual authors.

Cover Photo: Elizabeth DePriest from the collection of Rebecca Davis Henderson, Madison, Alabama, Elizabeth's first cousin once removed.
Elizabeth DePriest was the daughter of Nina and Robert W. DePriest, son of Turner DePriest and Martha Jane Hensley of Hickman County, Tennessee. In 1908, the family moved from Tennessee to Fresno, California for Robert's health. He wrote of his "loung" trouble improving there. He owned a confectionery and fruit business and sold Oliver typewriters in California. Robert passed away (tuberculosis) in Hickman, Kentucky (Nina's family home) on 3 January 1912. Elizabeth was married to Clayton Kiest Walser 17 July 1925 in Anna, Illinois.

ISBN 1-884289-28-2   9.95

FIRST EDITION: 2000
GRANDMOTHER EARTH CREATIONS
P. 0. Box 241986
Memphis, Tennessee 38124

"Circles in Nature: Mushroom Gill Pattern." by Neal Hogenbirk

*We hopefully will stop to consider
All the blessings we've had since birth;
One of the greatest God has provided
Is our home--Grandmother Earth.*
               -Embree Bolton

Grandmother Earth Creations was awarded the second annual Business Environmental Award by the city of Germantown, Tennessee Environmental Commission... for its pro-active role toward promoting environmental awareness by Sharon Goldsworthy, Mayor of Germantown.

Grandmother Earth Creations prints all books on recycled paper in accordance with their philosophy of helping to preserve the earth. Most of the customary blank pages are omitted.

Grandmother Earth VI Winners' List

Poetry Grand Prizes:
1st—"Wolf-wind," Kitty Yeager, Arkadelphia, Arkansas
2nd—"Against the Earth's Back," Frieda Dorris, Memphis, Tennessee
3rd—"When Monday Was Washday," Ann Hoffman, Ft. Smith, Arkansas
4th—"Letter to Dylan," Maureen Cannon, Ridgewood, New Jersey
1HM—"The Underside of Stones," Jane Davis Carpenter, Denver, Colorado
2HM—"Once in Mississippi," Winifred Hamrick Farrar, Meridian, Mississippi
3HM—"Still Not Quite Gone," Rosemary Stephens, Memphis, Tennessee

Humor:
1st—"Parking Lot Blues," Dodie Messer Meeks, Houston, Texas
1HM—"Oh, Foot, Let's Have a Ball," Malra Treece, Memphis, Tennessee
2HM—"Presidential Hopeful 2049," Russell H. Strauss, Memphis, Tennessee
3HM—"The Blessing," Eugene Shea, Hanna, Wyoming

Haiku:
1st—"the seaguls," Kolette Montague, Centerville, Utah
2nd—"clouded August moon," Glenna Holloway, Naperville, Illinois
3rd—"the barefoot boy," Leonardo Alishan, Salt Lake City, Utah
1HM—"The old dog," Kolette Montague, Centerville, Utah
2HM—"smoke cloud rising," Brett Taylor, Lancing, Tennessee
3HM—"in the oiran's hand," Leonardo Alishan, Salt Lake City, Utah
4HM—"courtyard of flowers," Elizabeth Howard, Crossville, Tennessee
5HM—"nest of hornets," Brett Taylor, Lancing, Tennessee

Environmental:
1st—"Kissing the Water, Wearing the Sun," June Owen, Zephyrhills, Florida
1HM--"This Is Not a Poem About a Tree," Barbara Brent Brower, Okemos, Michigan
2HM—"Protest," Elizabeth Howard, Crossville, Tennessee
3HM--"Time Travels," Nina Salley Hepburn, Cordova, Tennessee
4HM—"Arkansas – Approaching 2000 A. D." Annetta Talbot Beaucamp, Helena, Arkansas
5HM—"Blue Moon Vigil," Kolette Montague, Centerville, Utah
6HM—"Marjory Stoneman Douglas," Alice Heard Williams, Lynchburg, Virginia
7HM—"An Autumn High," Bettye K. Cannizzo, Decatur, Alabama
8HM—"When The Vultures Come Back to Lugar Del Muerte," James Hall, Pueblo, Colorado
9HM—"The Time of the Tiger," Barbara Brent Brower, Okemos, MI

Short Form:
1st—"Hollyhock Ballet," Dena R. Gorrell, Edmond, Oklahoma
1HM—"Sipping a Glass of Morning," Russell H. Strauss, Memphis, Tennessee
2HM—"Faith," Mabel Carver Taylor, Clearwater, Florida
3HM—"A Time to Harvest," Betty Heidelberger, Lexa, Arkansas
4HM—"White," Adams, Burlingame, California
5HM— "Few Words," Hollis K. Cathey, Ash Flat, Arkansas
6HM—"Triosphere," Jeanie Miller, Hanceville, Alabama
7HM—"T V Commericals, etc." Olga Warner Penzin, Waxhaw, North Carolina
8HM—"Advice From Uncle George," Sandra Lake Lassen, West Jefferson, North Carolina

Youth:
1st—"In Transit," Carolyn Moir, Lexington, Maine
2nd—"We," Carly Kiel, Memphis, Tennessee
3rd—"Autobiography of an Eleven-year-old," Rachel White, Memphis, Tennessee
1HM—"Forgotten," Radha Gajjar, Germantown, Tennessee

2HM—"Tomorrow," Jennifer Leigh Wheeler, Solona Beach, California
3HM—"In the Sky," Angelica DePrimo, Nesconset Elementary, Nesconset, New York
4HM—"That Day," Sarah Gosline, Howell, Michigan
5HM—"Wind," Eric Rogers, Memphis University School, Memphis, Tennessee

Editors' Choice: "Red," Marcia Camp, Little Rock, Arkansas

Prose Grand Prizes:
1st—"To Plodge in the Pacific," Christine Watt, Irvine, California
2nd—"The Bottom of her Feet were Pink," Janice Levy, Merrick, New York
3rd—"Hurrah, Hurrah," Susan Murphy, Birmingham, Alabama
1HM—"The Awkward Apple that Became The Perfect Plum," Victoria Hodge, Memphis, Tennessee
2HM—"Jehova Jireh, My Provider," Dorothy Hannah, Senatobia, Mississippi
3HM—"Deities," Christine Watt, Irvine, California
4HM—"April Sky," Elizabeth Brown Stambaugh, Little Rock, Arkansas
5HM—"Christmas Chrysalis," Rebecca Davis Henderson, Madison, Alabama
6HM—"The Man who Looked like Jesus," Jim Baum, Champaign, Illinois

Humor:
1st—"The Prayer," Altha Murphy, Imboden, Arkansas
1HM—"Shirley Learns about Beauty," Evelyn Foote, Memphis, Tennessee
2HM—"Me? The Golden Years," Kenneth and Jan Chastain, Big Sandy, Tennessee

Environmental:
"The Last Hook-up," Pug Jones, Hot Springs, Arkansas
1HM—"Queen of the Night," Martha McNatt, Humboldt, Tennessee

Editors' Choice: "Christmas Chrysalis," Rebecca Davis Henderson, Madison, Alabama

Inez Elliot Anderson Memorial Award for Residents of Alabama

Poetry:
1st—"Field Workers Singing," Madge Pfleger, Mobile
2nd—"A Cat Named Poem or is it a Poem Named Cat," Bettye K. Cannizzo, Decatur
1HM—"You Are My Thoughts," Esther O'Donald, Hamilton
2HM—"Sea, Stone, and Dreams," Mary E. Haliburton, Hope Hull
3HM—"Mind Streams," Jane E. Allen, Wetumpka

Prose:
1st—"Wartime Holiday," Auguste Black, Huntsville
2nd—"Christmas Chrysalis," Rebecca Davis Henderson, Madison

Money prizes and other finalist were selected for publication at the discretion of the editors. Only entries, which included written permission, were considered. However, due to the large volume of entries we were unable to include all worthy material. Work which expressed the themes of human values and environmental issues were given priority.

Judges:

Poetry: Clovita Rice, editor of *Voices International*
Prose: Florence Bruce, editor of *Writers on the River*

Special Awards:
Pat Laster
Michael Denington
Louise Gearin
E. Marcelle Zarshenas
Grandmother Earth Staff

"Yellowstone Falls," by Marilyn Califf. Reprinted from
The Pen Woman, NLAPW, Cover, April, 1999.
Used with permission of the artist.

AN ANALOGY: TIME AND WINE

When I open some days they taste flat
and I can shake them and turn the hours
all upside down, but still no bubbles, no tingle of carbonation
to burn the tongue ...
How good to find when uncorking
some clear unlabeled hour,
moments that fizz
and spill over the top
and conversation with distinctive bouquet
which I know I will want
to drink again ...

Clovita Rice

AGAINST THE EARTH'S BROWN BACK

On twilight evenings when cicadas sing
when shadows settle in on sandy loam--
I wear my young years like a wedding ring
and tiptoe down a turnrow leading home.

My reverie returns to shotgun shacks--
to cotton houses where white gold was stored,
where weary pickers weighed their heavy sacks
and deep-south culture breathed from every board

Upon the earth's brown back the farmhouse loomed,
a haven for the soul and for the heart
where clans united and young minds were groomed
with tools to face the world and stand apart

And so I use my tools to carve new stone
a place to feed my spirit and my bone.

Frieda Beasley Dorris

HAIKU

marmalade cat
windowsill
sunrise

Kolette Montague

YOU ARE MY THOUGHTS
WOLF-WIND

A rag moon silvers your hair, Old Squaw,
as canyon breath flaps the buffalo skins.
Your leather cheeks pale in sleep,
as though the Great Spirit calls you deeper,
deeper into night.

I remember your father,
Apache awesome in eagle feathers,
when I brought the spotted ponies.
I lost my speech when you appeared
in butternut fringe of beaded doe-skin
with baskets of your belongings.

Our moccasins followed the river
to a teepee in yellow ferns,
where we breathed a sweetness
on each other to the soft thunder of drums.
We ate thicket plums by full moonlight,
and your face was a fragrant waterflower
in my fruit-scented hands.

Now the frail firebird dies
across a hard copper sky,
and you moan on a prairie-grass mat.
If howling Wolf Wind comes tonight,
the mushroom snow in my pouch is swift,
I will follow you, Old Squaw.

Kitty Yeager

WHEN MONDAY WAS WASHDAY

White wind-whipped sheets whirled
Hobo into a barking frenzy, while
Mama rested, remembering bulging
baskets, now flapping in the morning
sun. On Monday, Mama's burdened washer
waltzed the linoleum as tales poured
like detergent, and Mama taught us
about rub-board days and lye soap.
Soon, little Mama scurried down the line
plucking pins from pink bag tied
around her waist, snapping them
onto bed sheets, towels, shirts, and dresses.
Pluck, stretch, snap, pluck, stretch, snap.
Washday, rhythm reigned while Harry
and I watched Mama trying to keep pace
with other housewives; her clothes less
than picture-perfect on the line.
Sunset saw her out again. Open, snap,
drop, open, snap, drop.
Sheets, towels, pillow cases folded
into one basket, clothes tossed in another
ready for ironing on Tuesday.

Now, heavy with honeysuckle, the gate
hangs by one hinge, creaking, waking
memories of Mama, in her gingham dress,
pushing it with her knee, hip-balancing
a basket of wet clothes. Peeling house-paint
once gleamed like a white, winter-moon
in the bucket, as Daddy stirred it
with a stick, and brushed it on
one stroke at a time. Wind-torn shingles
soar like pigeons in variegated grays,
and I see Harry and me perched
on the peak, clad in bib-overalls and nail

aprons, watching Daddy repair the roof.
Our swing is gone, stolen brand new, like the one before it. "They won't get this one," Daddy said, as he bolted it to the limb. Next time we returned from Grandma's, sap oozed from the oak's naked wound. The teeter-totter is here, still chained and cemented to the yard, a rust-brown monument to Daddy's ingenuity. Inside, windows flung wide, a hint of honeysuckle in the air,
      I am home again.
When Monday was washday.

Ann Hoffman

LETTER TO DYLAN

How else but "gentle into that good night"?
What other way but gentle when the strength
To rage has been exorcised by the rite
Of strangers, ministering, and by the length—
The terrifying length - of hours that creep,
Clock-faced, toward dusk and dinner trays, toward pills
And geriatric jokes and fitful sleep.
Who hears a whimpering? Upon the sills
The dusty leaves of philodendrons lie,
Reproachful. In the gaudy light of day
The curtains are too bright. Who hears a cry,
Or stops to wonder if the glib cliche
Offends, or if it's heard, or why the hands
Palms upward, lie so still? Who understands
What waiting is, the shape of fear? How might
They go? How else but gentle into night?

Maureen Cannon

*Dylan Thomas, "Do Not Go Gentle into That Good Night"

"Gull Talk," by Neal Hogenbirk

HAIKU

The seagulls –
all that commotion
over one clam

Kolette Montague

ONCE IN MISSISSIPPI

One Roosevelt fall, well after the dead days
of late summer with its wilting flowers,
my preschool brother and I rode high
on our last load of cotton
three miles to Snowden's gin.

Well after the time of miniature suns
 swinging from persimmon trees
festooned with caterpillar bags
(the year then in full decline
and sprinkled delicately with frost),
we passed, along the way,
trees flaunting scarlet and gold
(blazing maples and sourwoods,
golden hickories and oaks);
and passed stubbled fields
where crows rose cawing
from ghostly shocks of corn
while an ancient sadness lay
on windless air that blue October day.

At journey's end beneath a long shed
with the wagon drawn to a stop
exactly under the cylindrical maw of the gin,
my brother leaned toward the strong vacuum,
the cotton beneath him streaming toward it.
Watching in horror and yelling,
I grabbed his shirttail to snatch him back
and frightened the languid mules
who lurched the wagon forward
to throw us both under smothering cotton.

And now, a lifetime later,
that autumn day invades a night in spring.

Caught on the flying years
our episodic moments
flee farther and farther away
until time swallows them
beyond retrieval except in grieving minds.
Then on a quiet evening,
while feeling the wistful moments of springtime
when everything quickens,
hovering memories emerge from blue stillness
to wring our hearts.

And so, in this pregnant springtime
that autumn day comes back
with spooked mules, a startled driver,
a stifling struggle, the dusty smell of cotton:
Comes now, with fireflies darting like golden sparks in the
    dark,
while overhead one star trembles alone,
and a thrush throws notes in the purple woods.

It was springtime when my brother's last struggle ended...
and I could not save him.

Winifred Hamrick Farrar

Mississippi Poetry Society 1999 Award
Mississippi Poetry Journal

TIME TRAVELS

The road to my house travels past
a Super Wal-Mart,
Dillard's and Penney's
and umpteen other stores
like Office Max and Pier One Imports
and Tuesday Morning.
Some say its a six-lane shopper's paradise.
Then there's Applebee's, Red Lobster
and Outback, McDonald's, Taco Bell
and IHOP.
Fast food or slow food,
it's the dining room of the suburbs.
But yesterday
it was a narrow two-lane road
dotted by barns and barbwire fences
and front porch sitters
waving at passersby,
where a rooster could safely strut
across the road
to visit a neighboring hen house
on the other side.

Nina Salley Hepburn

PRESIDENTIAL HOPEFUL, 2049

Truman Adams Silverstar
Is only thirty-eight,
But in our e-mails we have seen
No other name of late.
First he earned a fortune
Shipping diapers by computer
In pastel poly-plastic.
Parents thought that they were cuter.
He built condos in Antarctica,
Designed two rocket cars,
And fought against pollution
Of the Grand Canal of Mars.
Now he's campaigned in sixty states,
And, just to hedge his bet,
He holds a rally every night
On the Internet.

Liz promoted peace accords,
And when the shelling ceased
Annexed twenty emirates
In the Middle East.
Then came dauntless Susan,
Then Hillary and Dee,
Who bailed out sinking Medicare
Till 2083.

There are voters nearing forty
Who since their lives began
Have not encountered this before:
Could it be true? In fifty-two,
We might elect a man.

Russell H. Strauss

Photograph by Marilyn Califf

KISSING THE WATER, WEARING THE SUN

Burchell's Zebras, African Savanna

In this still place of crested
Mousebirds and green mambas,
Where the air respires audibly,
I must be still, not let binoculars
Or camera rattle or cause reflections:
Zebras are coming to drink.

Light from setting, tumescent sun
Turns their white stripes,
The tasseled tips of manes
To color of apricots.
The pool in which their hooves
Submerge is dark but shallow,
Swirled with rings of light.
Watershadows move between
Their slender legs.
The water's round eye,
Its tight-edged gaze
Are all that matter now.
I close my eyes and let my mind
Slide in among the zebras,
Between their bulging bodies,
Slip myself thin as a reed
Between the ribs of one of them.
If women are pieces of Adam's rib,
I am no woman; I am part
Of the slants that mark the coats
Of zebras, part of their far-off gaze.
I set my camera aside.
It is enough to be alone with zebras,
To see their beautiful heads bob
In the close-to-evening air, to see
Their beautiful, mascaraed eyes
And their dilated nostrils smelling
The water, their velvet muzzles
Pushing the water, their soft lips
Siphoning the water, tasting the water,
Their soft lips kissing the water
That is wearing the sun.

June Owens

From: *The Atlanta Review*

PARKING LOT BLUES

Broccoli trembling, here I go
distractedly murmuring, to and fro,
Back and forth, row after row.
Twinkle, twinkle, little car.
I know I didn't park this far
but I haven't the foggiest where you are.
Are you on a toot or bender?
Loosely grinning with one fender
bending toward some metal gender?
Did a Mercedes sashay by
and give my little Ford the eye?
One headlight lit and chrome awry
are you headed for some bar?
Twinkle, honk, do something car
Oh, how I wonder where you are.

Dodie Messer Meeks

FEW WORDS

Sayings of yesteryear I read;
"Get there firstest with the mostest."
"I came, I saw, I conquered."
"Sighted sub, sank same."
I also can do that--I think.
"Wrote poetry, won award."

Hollis K. Cathey

OH, FOOT, LET'S HAVE A BALL

He said that Alabama beat Ole Miss
or else it was the other way around.
I said "That's wonderful"--a lucky guess.
He thought my judgment keen and quite profound.
He looked so pleased, as if he thought that I
could be a critic of athletic power.
"They're really great," I said. He breathed a sigh
of gratitude and praised the team an hour.
I can't recall if he preferred Ole Miss
or Alabama. But he said that he
admired my knowledge of the game. To this
remark I nodded understandingly.
I pressed my luck and blew it all, I fear,
when I asked him, "What were they playing, Dear?"

Malra Treece

TV COMMERCIALS, ETC.

"Seeing is believing,"
Was a saying true and wise.
But now computers change things so
You can't believe your eyes.

Olga Warner Penzin

PROTEST

I

All day, chain saws roar,
a neighbor's giant trees falling
like rotten snags in a windstorm:
oak, cherry, walnut, hickory.
I hear the creak of their protest,
the thunk of their passing.
Pileated woodpeckers fly about
screaming. I found the nest
last week, saw the fledgling
heads poking out. But they're
not the only creatures uprooted.
Looking for a flower pot
in the shed, I come up with a handful
of spitting fur--a red fox kit.
He nearly scares me to death,
but he's trembling, eyes fossils of fear.
I give him oatmeal and turn him
loose in a dogwood thicket.
He cowers down, surrounded.

II

Newscasters report spiked sequoias,
tree-sitters, a dead protestor.
I hear of endangered species,
a pygmy colony of microscopic plants,
dream of an explosion
of birds about the feeder, one
a grosbeak-sized yellow bird
with black markings, perhaps
extinct, or perhaps only

a vision of what might have been.
I see pictures of rare animals,
read of the dire outlook.

III

In the name of birds, foxes,
and tree-sitters, I plant a forest
in my fallow field--oak, cherry,
walnut, hickory--each pygmy sapling
a protest against clear-cutting.

Elizabeth Howard

"Shadows," © 1995 by Judith Baker Jones

ARKANSAS-APPROACHING 2000 A. D.

Millennium past Millennium I slept,
quietly and undisturbed -
unsculpted clay, waiting for conception
only rarely, shuffled gently
by the soft tread of an Indian moccasin -
those tracks smoothed carefully
so none could know that I was stirred.
Then I was born -
a brawling, squalling birth,
attended by men who tore me from Earth's womb.
They shaped me in their image
with axes, guns, and Bowie knives.
Now - as I grow -
they carve me still
with more sophisticated tools.
Bulldozers, spikes and drills
Scar my face with rails and concrete.

Go softly, Man, lest there be nothing left
to tell what beauty lay in your Creation.

Annetta Talbot Beaucamp

Grey shell-shaped mountain
sheds dots. Shadows move
forecasting storm.

Barbara Abbott

QUEEN OF THE NIGHT

Martha McNatt

On a hot and dry August morning, I was watering my back porch plants, including a most unattractive member of the cactus family with long thick rubbery leaves, randomly attached to sprawling branches. Some of the leaves had turned rusty from excessive heat, and some showed signs of being chewed upon by water seeking insects. For a year or two, I had been threatening this ugly monstrosity. Just a few days before, I had told it, "If you don't bloom this year, you are headed for the trash pile when winter comes."

A neighbor had rooted the plant from a leaf following a night when she invited a group of friends to join a midnight vigil, observing the opening of her Night Blooming Cereus. I had been introduced to the Cereus years ago, but the full impact of an opening failed to register with me. I think I became bored with it, and went to sleep before the full beauty emerged, but the fragrance and the mystical atmosphere surrounding the occasion had lingered in my memory for a long time.

The plant is a member of the cactus family, but it has been crossed with many similar plants. As a result, multiple varieties exist, including one native to the American West, which, for most of its life looks like a pile of sticks, but comes alive once a year to produce one fragrant white flower. Another variety, Honolulu Queen, produces a bloom ranging from twelve to fourteen inches in length, which if pollinated, grows a bright red fruit known as a strawberry pear.

The friend who rooted my plant identified it as "Epiphyllum Oxypetalum," whose common name is Queen Of The Night. Her records from the late seventies indicate it has most often bloomed during late September, but in 1993, bloomed on August 25, in the early morning hours.

The morning I had threatened the plant was on or near August 20. The morning of my story may have been August 25. My neighbor had instructed me to water it sparingly. She said it did not like wet roots. I was sprinkling the dust covered leaves when I received the shock of my plant growing life. There, hanging from an insect bitten leaf, was the closed and wilted remains of an overnight bloom. Its eight-inch stem was hanging limply, and the whiteness of the petals was enclosed in a pod of dull brown leaflets, grasping the pod like hundreds of miniature fingers. How could this have happened? I had waited almost six years for this night, and I had missed it! The summer heat had been oppressive. I had not expected a bloom until late September. I had watered quickly and obviously had ignored the impending bloom event. This excuse did not dull my anger at myself.

The bloom pods sprout out of the vein of a leaf, appearing at first like a small brown bud on a short stem. Each day the stem becomes longer and the bud becomes larger. Within about two weeks, the stem begins to turn upward. Thus is the clue that opening is near. When the brown fingerlings around the bud begin to reach outward and a small opening appears at the end of the bud, it is time to invite the neighbors for "opening night." I apologized to the "Queen" and promised her another winter on the sun porch, but this story has a happy ending. In mid-September, three more buds appeared. I watched and watered, but within two or three days, one of them fell away--then another. I was discouraged, but day after day, the remaining stem grew longer and the bud grew larger.

In late September, I was rewarded. A giant, perfect bloom opened, beginning about 8:00 P.M. and was fully open by 11:00. A heavy fragrance filled the air, and hundreds of yellow stamens inside the alabaster orb seemed to wave a greeting as I sat on the floor, flashlight in hand, not wanting to waste a minute of the life of this mysterious and unpredictable, plant.

Several legends and names surround the Night Blooming Cereus. One legend says that the yellow stamens form a cradle, and the pistil hangs over it like a star, giving rise to the name, "Christmas Flower." Growers who have kept records, report that buds usually appear on or near the date of a new moon. For this reason, the plant is sometimes called the Moon Goddess.

At this moment, I have several leaves; partially submerged in potting soil, waiting for a slip that will produce new plants. Not everybody is willing to wait six years for a bloom, but in my opinion, Queen of the Night is worth the wait.

"Night Blooming Cereus," by Martha McNatt

The Awkward Apple That Became
THE PERFECT PLUM

Victoria Hodge

Brandon, a handsome and quiet seventh grader in my middle school art class, usually worked on his art with little commotion. One day, however, I noticed his frustrations mounting as he attempted to blend his colors with his red and green colored pencils to create a nice red apple. I made my way to his front row desk to be available for encouragement.

Whenever I notice a student in distress over his art, I stay alert to the possibility that he might want to scribble it out. My students know that I encourage them, instead, to move over to another space and start again. This story will help explain why I do that.

In Brandon's distress he had, indeed, marked through his apple with a harsh curved motion. As I stilled his hand, I reminded him that we need not cross out the unfinished apple just because we are frustrated. I listened to his valid concerns and there were steps he could take to finish out the apple. Yet, he had chosen to judge his work prematurely. As he talked, I pondered the slash down the center of his apple. His errant slash seemed to me to be more like a perfectly placed crease on a plum than an angered attempt to blot the whole thing out. Could the difficult process of creasing a plum have been achieved in the midst of his fit of anxiety? I asked Brandon to dismiss for the moment his idea of an apple. If it could be any color he wanted it to be, could he see another type of fruit emerging in that shape?

I do not remember how long it took for him to see it, but when he envisioned a plum on his paper, his eyes lit up as the circuit of possibility connected. He laid down the green and red pencils and picked up the indigo and purple ones. Although apprehensive about spending more time on something he thought was ruined, he began to slowly apply soft, gentle strokes of blues over the red apple. By the end of the class period, Brandon's countenance was being lifted with renewed enthusiasm by the subtle transformation of his work.

For weeks he concentrated on putting very little pressure on the pencils. This allowed the rich layers of blue to intensify the creased and shaded areas. His classmates were responding favorably to the richness in the color of the plum. This motivated him even more to concentrate on the most difficult instructions in using colored pencils; that is, stay soft and go slow. A few weeks later, Brandon announced that he was finished.

Many times my students have heard me say that God does not wad us up and toss us away when our marks go awry. However, Brandon's plum impacts us still more than mere instruction could ever do. The plum was beautiful and the artistic accomplishment in the life of Brandon was memorable. But the deeper truths revealed in the process of that artwork are on going and profound.

The students in the class admired the brilliance in the color of the plum. Close to the stem, you can see a small area that reveals the red that was so frustrating to Brandon. That subtle redness reminds us that the red from the errant apple is what has given the blues in the plum richness and depth. We see in Brandon's plum an intensity that without the mistake of the apple would have been unlikely. Never would he have put so much red and especially green if he had planned to do a plum for his project. We see now that our mistakes may be the very paths God has chosen to intensify with richness, depth and brilliance His divine purpose in our lives.

When I see Brandon's plum, I am not reminded of a student's impatience. Instead, I see a plum that is richer in its brilliance than any plum I have ever tried to color. Only when I ask the artist how he achieved such depth, will I discover the story of the awkward apple. The story of the apple, that awkward source of anxiety for Brandon, becomes in the end, not the shame of the artist, but the glory of the plum. Brandon did not have an awkward apple. He had the perfect plum.

MARJORY STONEMAN DOUGLAS

She looked at nature through adoring eyes,
she touched each bloom in loving benediction,
she praised the heron's homeward flight,
the alligator nesting in quiet cove.
All creatures perfect in her gracious sight,
she took each one and held it to her heart,
embraced the Everglades in visionary sweep,
saw the dangers only man could bring.

Save it! her plea, save Florida's fragile world!
Preserve it as our children's heritage!
The sea cow, shepherding her young
beneath soft winds which kiss the gulls in flight,
the lumbering turtle hiding eggs in sand,
the lily floating in still waters of the swamp.
The base, the humble she counted of great worth,
prized the smallest shell, the weakest frog,
each cypress, every wetland fern.

And through her wisdom we become her heirs,
sentinels, vigilant to protect,
stewards of Florida's great gift,
our precious legacy, the Everglades.

Alice Heard Williams

THE WISHBONE WISH

Mother says, "Cousin Margaret
is too busy to marry."
Weekdays, Margaret wears a tailored suit
with a starched white blouse. High collar.
She sits at her computer as "the"
secretary for the high school principal.
Dark-rimmed glasses pinch her ivory-smooth face.
A number-two yellow pencil sprouts above her right ear,
the point always sharp.
Weekends and evenings, she runs the family farm
where she raises blue-ribbon Holsteins
and grooms fine horses.

Mother says, "Henry is a blessing."
Henry is here for the summer harvest.
With a smile on his face
and a book of poetry in his pocket
he brings passion into Margaret's life.
Now, for the first time, Margaret sees
the green in grass, the yellow in corn,
the red and white in peppermint.
Reading words of Emerson, Henry plucks
a rainbow from the sky, lays it at Margaret's feet.
Breathless, she says, "I see colors now."

They sit at the kitchen table,
challenge each other over a wishbone,
each tug for the winning length.
Henry says, "What's your wish?"
Margaret whispers, " It won't come true if I tell."

Henry waits for a full moon.
He proposes under a blossoming apple tree.
Margaret's voice is soft,

"I'm not sure, I need ... time."
Henry says, "I'll wait - for awhile."

Margaret buys yellow wallpaper. Twelve single rolls.
No flowered print. No border.
She orders more garden seeds. Adds ten new rows.
She returns red barn paint, buys white instead.
The school urges Margaret to work more hours.
She consents.

At night, Margaret sits in her rocker,
rubs her eyes and wrinkled hands.
A sound breaks her reverie,
quick, clean, absolute ...
like the snapping of a wishbone.
The noise draws her from her chair.
A latch clicks ...
There is a squeak as a gate closes shut.
Margaret looks through the kitchen window
but the glare from the setting sun
won't let her see colors anymore.

Arla M. Clemons

HAIKU

The old dog
chooses her place in the dust
without circling.

Kolette Montague

GRANDPARENTS

Feet firm on the overturned box
Alice pressed the heavy rolling pin,
whittled oak log
rolling dough into soda crackers.
Alice Ashley, syllables like bird song
the only light to lift her spirits
beyond morning chores and endless
sisters and brothers, a chain
she thought her own marriage
would break, years in her Tennessee
mountain home traded for years
in a Kentucky mining camp,
hardscrabble soil for black
coal-dusted ground.

Bert, a man of banjo music
and quick, dancing steps,
a man tall as the mountains.
How could she know
his body carried a dark vein of desire
alcohol would ignite,
a wild nature years
underground could not tame.
She scrubbed his coal-encrusted clothing,
boiled pots of beans and potatoes,
bore his children, buried two babies,
until the day he ran off,
another woman's flaming hair
a lure strong as drink.

Years later, when he returned,
Alice gave him the back bedroom
where he slept propped against pillows,
his blackened lungs rasping through the night.

She cooked and cleaned for him,
slept in the front room, children at her feet,
found song only in the mountain church,
hymns heavy as pots, pans, rolling pin.

Connie Jordan Green

RED

is the flesh of burst watermelons
splayed on vendors' tables,
pouring their juice on Jerusalem's streets
when the market place
explodes with suicide bombs,
rains bricks and stones.
Red are the wounds of Israelis,
confirming a transient peace.

... and Abraham begat Ishmael with Hagar
... and Abraham begat Isaac with Sarah,
one a handmaiden, the other a wife.

From innocent couplings in
ancient desert tents
sprang two nations,
then love begat hate, and now
the streets of their holy city
run red.

Marcia Camp

THIEVES AND WINGS

I squat in front of Roscoe, as close to
eyeball to eyeball that I can get, see
the ridge of her ribcage, see
the hollow bowl shape of what
has become her stomach:
I feed and feed her, she
eats and eats and eats but
the cancer eats faster

I say to her what has become
a mantra for me:
I'll never let you go, Roscoe Picasso

she licks my cheek so gently
that it is like a kiss from a butterfly
before it flits away

Lise Kelley

Life is like a gem
Thoughts crystallize in our minds
My knees touch the floor

AnneMarie Dyer

Photograph by McLaurin Smith-Williams

Nest of hornets
alive with buzzing
leaning chimney

Brett Taylor

"Statue of Liberty," by Alice Garrison

AN UPDATE FOR EMMA LAZARUS

An Update for Emma Lazarus
"Give me your tired, your poor, your huddled masses yearning to breathe free." Emma Lazarus from "The New Colossus"
Emma Lazarus, daughter of Manhattan
Whose words are inscribed at the skirts of Liberty,
Can you image what has become
Of the children of your huddled masses

Who rolled into this great harbor
Like a human tidal wave
That spilled into the sweat shops
And flooded the tenements on Delancey Street?
What has become of the heritage
Of Sligo lads who fled the famine
To rivet trestles on the Brooklyn Bridge,
Of Lubavitcher urchins whose side-curls
Bounced as they played stickball on the curb.
Of the ginger and ginseng merchants on Pell Street
Who once were stowaways from Nanking,
Or of Enrico who took night classes
So he could pledge allegiance to America
And vote for La Guardia?
Their children have taken their legacies
Into the towers of Central Park West
And beyond to Long Island and Westchester;
Yet, even today, New York
Remains your golden door
And to watch the passers-by on Fifth Avenue
Is to look into the myriad faces of the world.

Russell Strauss

HAIKU

Fog greys the morning
stretching the depth of silence,
hanging in mid-air.

Florine Petkoff Walters

CONTEMPLATION

I am standing in my shadow
abandoned
I cannot erase the maze
How to deny to myself the drowning thoughts
that saturate every fiber
The future is akin to a complex mathematical challenge,
Solutions obliterate with confusion and defeat
Tear ducts arid.
A brief momentary interlude hovers beyond reach
only to vanish
Trapped in a body fraught with medical challenges
inevitable complexities
I accept what appears my fate
Yet—
A glimmer deep inside is at war with mind and body,
How to grasp this ray of hope
to cling and grow.

Rita Lurie

Olive green water
intercepts the sun before
lapping cool shadows.

Sandra O. Hancock

STILL NOT QUITE GONE
For Margaret Mitchell

We still pretend the plantations are ours
or were if those times could return
we would dance all night, laced tight in
lace and crinolines, by candles lit by those
hands we think so eager to serve us.
On high mahogany poster beds rising to
higher imported ceilings, we would sleep
all day, awakened briefly by cardinals,
by magnolia branches beating on our
heavy-sweet windows, velvet draped, and by
a golden giant, divested of his sword and
boots and sash, climactically parting
our bed-muslin curtains, his smile as light
as the feathers packed beneath us, bending
now like a sea under his bent knee.
When today we drive through the countryside past
unpainted houses, some deserted as the fields
surrounding them, silent as seas long dead,
old cotton stalks seaweed-littering the dirt,
we know the gleam of distant columns.
Even when the houses aren't deserted and
faces watch us past canna lilies in cans,
we ignore the multi-colored washing strung on
porch railings and fences, ignore that single
mulberry tree where mockingbirds repeat old songs.
Even as we hear Slattery voices, we think of the
Wilkes' soft tones, the touch of something never felt,
felt always, waiting in our longing, perhaps
beside this next magnolia, beyond this next bend.

Rosemary Stephens

From *BARBEQUE PLANET, Contemporary Poets of the New South.*

THE VISITOR

If I knock at your door too much,
Or dial your telephone,
If you don't like to see me come
And wish I'd stay at home,

Please try to understand my need
to sit with you a while,
To hear a word of welcome and
To see a friendly smile.

There's no one in the house with me
I live alone, you know
There's nothing on TV to watch
And I can't read or sew.

I won't stay long, I promise.
I will soon be on my way
And God will bless the little time
You spend with me today.

Martha L. Carpenter

Saffron golden leaves
Stirring in the gentle wind;
    Time's slow clock moves on.

John W. Crawford

AUTUMN OMENS

Magnolia's untimely bloom
Accents these abbreviated days,
Maple leaves stir restless
In their space until they fling
Their single shadow from my shade;
Lulled by cicada's hum
A sluggish, brown grasshopper walks
Among sky scraping stalks of golden rod,
Seeds made, frost hovers a breath away,
Today a writing spider wrote my name—
Such omens hang my yearning hopes
On days that number into spring...

Burnette B. Benedict

THE SUN IS AN ORANGE

The sun is an orange full of music
Flowing as a harp's strings
To connect the firmament with the earth
Playing
       flowers
             butterflies
                   sparrows

Kareem Al-Darahi

CHILD'S PLAY

It looks like a toddler tornado has played Pickup Sticks
    with trees and then
dumped fireplace ashes all over the mess in a tantrum.
My black Lab can't even vault the hurdles.
But I remember when even my born-lame wheel-carted cat
    used to be able to make it down this old golf course
    path
    behind our house.
I know what they're doing, these guys
    with mansize backhoes and earthmovers.
They feel like they're back in the sandbox.
It's fun to poke and burrow, toss and dump.
But it's also grownup heady to re-arrange the landscape.
Arid use matches to eat away the tree trash
I'm sure it's flat exciting, too, to know that at the end of the
    day,
    there'll be more than Snickerdoodles
    as reward for the day's occupation:
They *know* that what they're dredging up can be trucked off
    and sold for mansize money.

But the dog and I miss the rabbits that used to tempt him
into the woods.
And the deer that left tracks for him to circle near the mini-
lakes left by the rain.
And the sparrows and mockingbirds he loved to scatter and
bark to.

Now there aren't even any occasional buzzard shadows.
And the sky seems too big with the trees on their backs.

Sherry Organ

THE TIME OF THE TIGER

Are we saying the time of the tiger is over;
the time of the whale, of the wolf,
the time of the sea otter...over?

Are we saying the time of the panda has passed;
that the loss of whole classes of fish
are insignificant in the face of the progress we've made?

Are we saying we no longer need our great rain forests;
that man can make clean air from smog?
Are we saying that man, alone, deserves saving?

Do we really believe we can replace all that's been lost
with chemical magic and miracle clones;
be happier when children have only photograph-forests
      to roam?

And when we have finished dismissing
every thing living but man,
will we stand at the edge of some desolate sea,
devoid of shells and sweet calls of birds,
crying, like spoiled children over toys
we have thoughtlessly broken,
and mumble a mantra that will never be answered:
We are sorry, we will change, please return?

Barbara Brent Brower

DELTA SLEUTH

Thrusting through Post Office door,
I brush a blonde, shampoo fresh—
she'll drive the Land Rover.
Another, coat hanger-thin
in perfume cloud and power suit,
spikes her way to her box.
The red Lexus will be hers.

The man with honey-colored skin,
confident in Italian suit,
radiates a faint spice,
ancient and mysterious as his origins.
His Ferrari defiantly
purrs at the curb
(no one steals from such a man).

My box key releases a tobacco smoke
potpourri—each brand promising
virility or glamour.
I drive to work with
open windows scooping
burnt sugar off
drive-in sweet rolls.

The white line reels me back to Delta smells—
skunk (bitter, acrid, almost a taste),
lush rotting vegetation, lazy buzzard feasts,
fear-infusing musk of snake—
for I am as much a child of the earth
as an aborigine
chasing the scent of rain.

Marcia Camp

A DITTO FOR WHICHEVER SEQUENCE

at the day of your last roses
encircled in a mist of mortals
blooming ritual
I am naked
in this pew splintered
with having lived
with living
my soul is naked ... who notices?

these mourners minding mourning
wear no raised eyebrows

at the smile of final dialogue
who designates play labels?

flesh to spirit ... spirit to flesh
I loved you ... love you
and though ... perhaps invisible
inaudible
this is the only rose
I have

Ruth Peal Harrell

MOSQUITO HAWKS

Dragonflies whirl across the pond:
An army of helicopters go to war.

Margot Marler

"Opening Sunflower I," by Neal Hogenbirk

Summer's flowers bold;
Colors flourish in the heat
Of the steamy day.

Jennifer A. Jenson

A TIME TO HARVEST

Autumn
spreads her fingers
to catch the last harvest
before winter cold turns ripe fields
to ice
      Betty Heidelberger

WHITE

white, white,
white fairy flowers,

spare brown limbs
shining in spring rain

frame the fragrant blossoms
on an aged cherry tree

Adams

HOLLYHOCK BALLET
(Cinquain)

Slender
ballerinas
costumed in pink tutus
swirl and dip and sway in summer
breezes.

Dena R. Gorrell

steeds leap to the whip
multi-roofed temples stand
throngs flock to worship

Edith Guy

    the barefoot boy
    delivering a bucket of coal
    in the night snow

    Leonardo Alishan

An astonishing
sonnet awaits inside a
multihued sunset

La Vonne Schoneman

        dogwoods dye their leaves
        crimson red for Halloween
        autumn masquerade

            Evelyn C. Foote

blue afternoon
looking up at the sky
no shapes left there

Brett Taylor

ON HIGHWAY 90 IN SOUTH DAKOTA

Highway 90, flat and straight,
Is history on a treeless, grassy, horizon?
Turned Westward, in sunset's glow, we watch
Sheets of thunderstorm unravel
In threads of jagged light. Until,
Still fifty miles out in the silence,
Rapid City twinkles to us in the darkness.
Outside our windshield, wheezing to us,
Are ghosts of buffalo, of Custer's Seventh
Cavalry, of Crazy Horse and his betrayed
Lakota. Sable shrouded ghosts
Of the slaughtered lament to us. They moan
To the passing moon-calves not far from
The invisible sacred Black Hills.

J. Richard Hancock, Jr.

MORNING GLORY

A gauze curtain embraces
the golden autumn colors.
The soul is in a trance--
Slowly the sun rises
as silver drops.

Margot Marler

A SONG TO MY HUSBAND

We pause beside a koi* pool and we
Observe our images reflected there,
As multi-colored koi rise to see
Our hugs and hear our laughs, a scene so rare
They watch awhile. It was not always thus.
We each explored the other and were pleased,
Yet other avenues attracted us
And we pursued diverse affairs. Love eased
Our way and blossomed, lush and lovely and
We were surprised, delighted. Koi eye
Us now and see our faith that could withstand
The years; the hope that would refuse to die.
Though soon you'll leave and I'll be left forlorn,
Your love will lift me, guide me as I mourn.

Patricia W. Smith

*Koi are large, multi-colored fish of the carp family similar to goldfish. The Japanese believe that they are endowed with mystical qualities.

in the *orion's* hand
a Japanese fan
her hand finer than the fan

Leonardo Alishan

THE RED WINGED BLACKBIRD OF SHELBY FARMS

Out where I live there is a road
that takes me home
through a farm with green pastures,
little lakes and shady trails
alive with duck, birds, geese,
lakes of Bream, Bass, and Catfish,
Great Herons and small Killdeers.
What a shame to spoil
quiet beauty, pristine grace
with highways of gaseous smells,
rattling trucks.
I hope that I can always see
the Red Winged Black Bird take flight
among the peaceful fields.

Gayle Fleming Hulsey

Written to support the struggle to keep the five thousand green acres of Shelby Farms Park, Memphis, Tennessee, free from industrial encroachments.

courtyard of flowers
    pygmy parrots hop about
      eating papayas
(Venezuela)

Elizabeth Howard

THIS MOMENT

I lie here lonely on this full-moon night,
Without your arms to keep me company;
Regretful of a love that once was bright,
A torch that lit a heart that was not free...
Where are you this moment?
Does strolling
down some other
avenue ...
Make you forget our low-tide secret shore...
Or does this moment hold your racing heart,
With feelings that you never knew were there?
I lie here lonely on this full-moon night.

Patty Hoye Ashworth

THE CRYSTAL SEASON

Ice-blue winter sky
over blinding rigid white.
Sharp, stinging wind.
Rascal crows on gray, bare limbs:
Glacier, Montana.

Margot Marler

THE UNDERSIDE OF STONES

This stone came from Oregon's coast;
A small Henry Moore sculpture it is,
Hole like a window through which to see
A different world. Two smaller stones
Cling to the hollow, having clung
Through tides both ebb and flow,
Their bottoms serrated like teeth.

If you have ever walked upon a beach
Along the coast of Oregon, you know
Why this tenaciousness. No soft sand
Takes your footprint; it is one stone
After another, ranging from pebbles
To boulders--take care walking there.
Now, this one beckoned from a posted
Falling Rock Zone--serendipitous because
Its mica brightness beaconed out
From an otherwise indistinguishable
Heap. That it survived the rockfall
Is a wonderment. It flakes, you see,
Unlike the hardier specimens, built up
From strata, visible layers of time.
But how can one resist it? It shines
So in the sunlight, and it fits just
Right into a jeans pocket to take home.
Set in the side garden, it need know
No more harsh traveling, and can endure.

Finally, my favorite stone. You see
This fish, its bony shape imprinted
Like a petroglyph? It tells us in
A literal translation that once,
Eons ago, where we stand was ocean,

Or glacier melt, or a great flood ...
The underside is smooth as an egg,
Another sign that water has washed it.

I look at this fish fossil and think
How children form snow-angels,
Making their bid for immortality
(When this you see, remember me).

But sun melts angels made of snow.
And stones let fall can shatter history.

Jane Davis Carpenter

THE MIRROR

How frightened I was
when she looked at me.
Eyes fallen deep into blue,
skin pale as snow,
lines of worry so profound,
hair silver from age.
Yet her expression that of a child
reflecting from my mirror.

Margot Marler

DRIFTING AWAY

That windowpane of sky
textured with clouds,
from washday lights to darks,
wings me away
from these bedridden days,

They're never quite the same,
  those clouds:
marshmallow
  frosted with peacock,
cumulus with
  gilded bellies
and <u>buttermilk</u> clabber
  ridged with lilac
float past that window.

Sometimes they weep
but I keep scanning
my piece of sky because
one day I, like Moses,
will follow a pillar of cloud
that will lead me
  out of my wilderness.

Verna Lee Hinegardner

From *Hearts of the South*

WHERE IT CAME FROM

Rage uncontrolled, rampant in my soul.
Shameful hurtful misdirected.
Why such fear for the uniform of
a cop? He too wore the uniform.
He was my cop.
With a police special cold held to my head.
I wish I'd made him use it.

I saw him first in pictures, held before my baby face.
He wore a hat and uniform
American soldier that served on foreign shores.

He came back to live with me
and brought his livid anger.
But I saw the uniform before I saw his face.
Somewhere deep inside of me my fear turned
to vivid hate.

Who can hate their father?
The man makes up half of me.

He came from behind to strip and rape my soul.
I saw the face of a cop, the picture on the wall
who wore a uniform and hat, and wouldn't stop.

The things he did to me weren't really done by him,
but by the face on the wall, and I became a them.

I want to rip his head off, reach into his gut
pull the organs from his shell
step on them, feel them squish
between my toes.
Hold his heart in my hands
and peel away the layers, linger
while the life of him runs warm on
my finger.

I wouldn't let him live to know,
at last, at the very longest
last, I KNOW. I KNOW. I am mad
filled with a black dreadful fury, so terrible
I can't let it show.

Come back from the dead old man
and try to take me on.
Come young and big and mean
I want to hear you scream.

You will find a daughter growing
stronger everyday waiting now to find
her own very special way to repay you in kind,

show you how pain racked my life.
Tell you just before I'd kill you, how I still
love you so, and how I hate me
for letting that sick, sick weakness grow.

If I could kill you then maybe
I could kill the pain in me or at least kill the
you in me I see.

Ruth Rakestraw

SPRING OF LIFE

I saw a yellow field of life
Where there was no drum roll and fife.
Yet there was music everywhere
While butterflies fluttered here and there

Gloria R Lee

TO PLODGE IN THE PACIFIC

Christine Watt

I kidnapped my mother-in-law that California morning and fled out of Los Angeles down Pacific Coast Highway 1. I didn't know where we were going exactly, but I knew I was taking her to the beach. I had decided that what Mama needed was to dip her toes in the healing waters of the mighty Pacific.

Mama proved a willing participant in this gang-land style abduction. Her spirits had been desperately low at the prospect of having a toxic soup of chemicals pumped into her yet another sunny day. While we couldn't speak each other's native tongue, we had conspired to outwit her daughter, with some help from Jamie who speaks both Farsi (Persian) and English.

I selected a solitary place. Mama needed nature's peace and quiet, the plaintive cries of gulls and the pounding of blue and white surf in her ears, not blaring traffic, yammering humans, and sterile, metallic hospital noises. Jamie consulted the map. If we stuck to Pacific Coast Highway 1, he assured me, we were bound to find somewhere. And as we curved out of Newport Beach, we did. Suddenly before us, the vast ocean glinted like a metal sculpture carving the land into a perfect crescent.

"*Bah, bah,*" murmured Mama. "'Oh my, oh my."

The sparkling bay stretched deserted below us. I pulled into the first parking lot I came to. "Crystal Cove State Park" the sign said. As if to bless our playing hooky, a Swallowtail fluttered onto the white hood of the car and took a breather, yellow and blue wings flapping in the intense, hot light. Mama's face glowed like a little girl's on Christmas morning. I grinned at Jamie, who giggled. We hadn't seen Mama's face so animated for months. We waited for the butterfly to resume her journey; then Jamie and I yanked the wheelchair out of the trunk and helped Mama into it. Drowning in dancing pink and lavender wildflowers, we headed off into a piercing sun down a Tarmac® path winding steeply down the cliffs.

Once we arrived at the beach, the wheelchair presented problems, but Mama laughed out loud as we bounced her over gray pebbles to the tide-line of dried seaweed and on to flat, moist sand recently bathed by the tide. We parked near an outcrop of boulders, Jamie flinging himself flat on his back onto them.

"These rocks are so warm," he moaned, as comfortable as a cat.

Mama gazed out to sea, and my heart warmed to see golden light reflect off silver waves onto her deeply smiling face. "*Bah, bah,*" she mumbled and reached for my hand. We sat holding hands a long time, just watching the ocean. Although I'd been raised in England on the shores of the bleakly beautiful North Sea, the untamable Pacific has truly captured my heart.

As the tide ebbed, I spied tide pools. "Hey, Jamie."

So relaxed he was practically melting, all Jamie could manage was a grunt in reply.

"You ever seen tide pools?" I asked.

He bolted upright. Sea creatures fascinated my city-bound nephew; I'd taken him to one of those IMAX® movies about sharks weeks ago, and he hadn't stopped talking about it yet. "Tide pools," he repeated in wonder.

I pointed to islands of brown-green seaweed.

"Wha-a-a-a," he yelled, leaping off the boulder.

"Tell Mama we're just going to have a wander over there."

Jamie crouched beside his grandmother and explained to her. She stroked his curly, black hair in reply.

I pounded down the beach to crash through foam to the rocks.

"Wait," Jamie shrieked, hopping about on one foot as he yanked off enormous sneakers.

I turned to wave to Mama, who waved back. It pained me to see how much effort that simple motion ate up.

"Do you think Mama would like to plodge?" I asked Jamie.

"To what!" He bent like a hairpin over a puddle of tiny crabs, who scuttled away from his shadow to hide under curtains of pungent seaweed. Plump, squat anemones the color of bruised flesh

55

wafted their tendrils in the crystal clear water, a hearty soup for them no doubt.

"It's an English word, as opposed to an American one, for dipping your toes at the edge of the sea," I explained.

He glanced over his bronzed shoulder back to Mama, a little old lady swathed in a black shawl, she looked so frail. Eyes sparkling, he beamed at me. What a heart-breaker my young nephew would be one day.

We splashed through the waves, then cut up the beach. Before Jamie had even finished explaining to her, Mama had impatiently unwound her shawl and was lifting her feet off the wheelchair footrest.

I kneeled to remove her velveteen slippers, and she nodded with glee.

Jamie and I pulled her up and waited for her to feel secure. She took a deep breath, focused on the distant horizon, and out shot one small foot. The slope wasn't of any consequence to Jamie and me, but Mama's toes groped before she dared venture each step. She almost toppled a couple of times, and I regretted my idea as I saw her breathing labor, but she gritted her jaw. She couldn't vanquish the cancer, but she could and would do this.

As soon as icy spume flooded between her toes, her body melted, yet Jamie and I were able to move slightly away as she stood on her own. Eyes closed, Mama tilted her face to the sun and breathed deeply. As her lungs let go of that cleansing air she moaned a soft sigh of such contentment, my eyes scalded with tears.

We arrived back in L. A. after dark, sneaking into the apartment like three naughty mice. My sister-in-law was frosty, what on earth had we been thinking of? Mama, Jamie, and I exchanged conspiratorial glances. We knew.

At bedtime, I pressed my face to Mama's sun-kissed cheek and wished her a good night.

She winked.

THE PRAYER

Altha Murphy

Whew! That was a close call! I hope I never get in a jam like that again.

The time was the early 30's. It began as I played under two big oak trees between our front yard fence and the road. During hot weather I spent a lot of time playing there in the shade.

A car had been under the trees for a few days. A Whippet, they called it. It belonged to Mr. Marshall, the man who owned the ground we rented. We had forty acres of our own, but that wasn't enough to support a family of five.

My folks were considering buying the car, so Mr. Marshall left it there a few days while they made the decision. We had never owned a car. My two big brothers were hoping we took it. Me, too. It would be so much faster than walking or going by wagon.

Earlier that afternoon, I checked to see if anyone happened to be watching. No one was, so I opened a door and hopped in the back seat. You know, just to get the feel of it in case we did buy it. The seat was all clean and soft, ever so comfortable. Turning around, I noticed a window shade on the back window. Hm-m-m, that was interesting. It had fringe on the bottom and a little ring to put your finger in. I wasn't familiar with window shades. Our windows in the house had curtains made of sacks, all starched and ironed, but no shades. I gave the tiniest yank. The shade moved down a bit and stopped. That was fun! One more little pull couldn't possibly hurt anything, could it?

After a few more little tugs, the shade plopped all the down, even past the bottom of the window and onto the back of the seat. Oh, my! I wasn't prepared for that. I would have to give it a sharp pull and let it fly back up. Even after several sharp pulls it didn't move a bit.

Now it was time to worry. What if the shade never went back up? What kind of trouble would I be in then? More than likely, Mama would give me a dose of her peach tree tea (swats across the legs with a little peach tree branch). Worse still, Papa might give me one of his talks. And Mr. Marshall --What would he do? I wondered if they put little kids in jail for stuff like this. I had never heard of one being jailed. But then, I also had never heard of a kid ruining someone's car.

I thought maybe I could pray about it. I had heard a song on the radio about a royal telephone. I had also heard Mama sing it as she worked. It went something like this:

> Central's never busy, always on the line.
> You can hear from heaven almost any time.
> Built by God the Father for His very own,
> You can talk to Jesus on this royal telephone.

I felt a pressing need to use that telephone, but I only knew one prayer. It was one I said before going to bed at night. It went like this:

> Now I lay me down to sleep.
> I pray the Lord my soul to keep,
> If I should die before I wake,
> I pray the Lord my soul to take.

I wasn't really pleased with that part about dying before I woke. But since that was the way the prayer went, that's what I said.

We had a big picture on the wall over my bed with a little boy and his big dog kneeling by the bed, saying their prayers. I often wondered if that boy said the same prayer I did.

At any rate, I didn't feel that prayer fit the predicament I found myself in with the shade. So I forgot about rhyming words and memorized lines. I began talking directly to God, begging Him to get me out of that mess, and to please hurry, before someone caught me. I promised Him if He would make that window shade go up, I would do anything He wanted me to.

When I finished talking on the royal telephone, I gave the shade one more yank. Miracle of miracles, it rolled up on that roller and snapped into place as if it had always been there. I got out of the car and shut the door. No one could tell by looking that I had ever been in it.

That night at supper Papa announced that he was not buying the car. It seemed we couldn't afford it. At that point, I didn't even care. I was so relieved that my prayer was answered, I didn't care if I had to walk everywhere I went from that day forward.

No one knew that I had been fooling around where I had no business. No one, that is, except God--and He wasn't telling!!!!

SIPPING A GLASS OF MORNING

A creme de cacao night was served
Before the robust wine of dawn.
A million tipsy sunbeams
Are tottering across my lawn.

Russell H. Strauss

THE BOTTOM OF HER FEET WERE PINK

Janice Levy

My mother was not from the cooks. Her measuring cups were chipped, her pots dented, her pans blackened and bruised. She used the bottom of her shirt as a potholder. When she burned or cut herself, she'd give a yelp, but never put on a band-aide. She was always in a hurry –

While my mother cooked, I spun on a rusty stool, my legs kicking a counter, and watched "The Mike Douglas Show" on our black and white T.V. Sammy Davis Jr. danced to "Mr. Bo Jangles." My mother fried the meat patties until they looked like charred shipwreck, then plopped them on a paper plate where canned peas and carrots swam. I had to eat fast, before my dinner sprung a leak.

My mother unhooked the safety pin cinching her waistband and ate standing up, digging her hand into a box of Ritz crackers. When my father's car pulled into the driveway, she swept the crumbs into a corner and pushed bobby pins through her kinky hair. "Next shift," she announced, but I stalled, squishing my Ring-Ding and picking it apart, until Mike finished singing, "The Men In My Little Girl's Life." And I wished again for a father who would cry over me or who at least could carry a tune. …..

My father sat at the table on a cushioned chair and ate off a real plate; his peas and carrots were even hot. But still he griped, scratching his stomach like a bear. "Again no napkins? No ketchup? No fork?" My mother scurried back and forth like a kitten on glass.

My father gave me the change in his pockets, then waved me away; he said he liked to hear himself chew. While he grunted into his newspaper, my mother leaned against the stove, dipping Orioes into black coffee. She didn't split them open to lick off the cream. Until she shooed me out of the kitchen, I watched her watching my father and swallowing her cookies whole, like a snake.

My family didn't "do" Thanksgiving. As far as I knew, you did Thanksgiving only if you were a Pilgrim or could cook like Uncle Charley on "My Three Sons." But when I was six, my father invited his boss to Thanksgiving dinner at our home.

"We never--" my mother protested. "Really, Richard, you don't even like turkey." She picked at her cuticles. "I don't have what to wear."

My father suggested a flour sack. He was more concerned with his boss choking on a bone or the roaches carrying away the food. He said my mother cleaned with her eyes shut.

I said I'd dress up as a Pilgrim and mash cranberries in the bathtub with my feet. I danced with a broom and flapped my arms like a turkey. My mother reached for a bag of chips. My father massaged his forehead. Then he opened the Yellow Pages and called "the agency."

Though I'd never met Dora-from-the-agency, I knew she had to be someone important, because my mother taped tissues around the toilet seat and copied down the license plate numbers of Dora's car. I was puzzled, though, when my mother hid her gold watch in a Cheerios box and followed Dora from room to room as she cleaned. "She smells," my mother told my father." He said Dora had a nice ass.

Dora sang to the turkey as she rubbed it with spices. She taught me how to roll out dough for the apple pie. I traced my hand on construction paper and colored the fingers like turkey feathers. Dora didn't yell when I spun across the floor in a big wooden salad bowl. I asked her why the bottoms of her feet were pink, and she said the skin had rubbed off from so much standing. I laughed when she took out her front teeth. Dora braided my hair and stopped a run in my stocking with clear nail polish. She said I was the prettiest Jewish girl she'd ever seen, and that my nose wasn't even that big.

"Dora," my mother said, "you'll do the dishes after the company's gone." Then she squeezed my arm. "Don't you come downstairs until you're called."

Dora and I sat on the floor in the corner of my bedroom, picking up the conversation through the heating vent. "Your wife's quite the little lady, isn't she?" the boss said. "You must have slaved all day," his wife said to my mother. "Everything is just perfect."

I asked Dora why she didn't go downstairs and tell them the truth. She said there wasn't any point in trying to take credit, because you could wait a lifetime for them to give it to you, and she'd rather have the time of her life than wait a lifetime, any day. Then she told me to name all the things I was thankful for, and when I got stuck after Mike Douglas, my fish Goldie, and Twinkies, she said I should be thankful it was the turkey in the oven and not me.

Dora and I had our own Thanksgiving. We ate an entire box of Malomars, picking off the chocolate shell and scraping our teeth against the graham-cracker bottoms, then stuffing the marshmallows into each other's cheeks.

"Happy Thanksgiving," Dora said, and she gave me a sip from a bottle she'd taken from my parents' "keep-out" closet. I asked her to wake me when they called for me to say my 'How-do-you-do's.' Dora smiled, then took off my glasses and kissed the part of my face that nobody ever touched.

Transiting crag floes,
Graceful yacht in grinding fields,
Liquid abatoir.

Thomas W. McDaniel

THE LAST HOOKUP!

A.H. "Pug" Jones

Jim Harding was as excited as a seven-year-old on Christmas morning.
"Want some breakfast?" asked his wife, Lynne.
"No thanks, Hon, I've had coffee and juice. See you tonight," he said and kissed her cheek.
"OK, have fun." He was on his way. Today was June 3, 2118. He and his friend, Bill, were going fishing. It was an hour's ride to their destination. A small ice chest held sandwiches, sodas and two fishing lures that he'd thrown in for old time's sake. Downtown, Jim got off his tram, smiling at his reflection in a store window.

When Bill's express tram came, he was wearing fishing vest and floppy hat, dry flies hooked to its brim. *All that's missing are his waders*, Bill thought. "Morning, Jim."
"Hey, Bill. You ready?"
"Ra'aring to go."

Once on the throughway, conversation stopped. The sun was up and the fields seemed greener than usual, even when viewed though the constant yellow haze. Mile markers zipped by. Finally, Jim broke the silence. "Bill, remember, when we went fishing on Loon Lake, thirty years ago? Lynne thought I didn't love her anymore, because we were newly-weds and I went fishing."

Bill nodded. "What a day that was. Sunny, no wind, and fish so hungry, we stayed busy just unhooking 'em."
"Yeah, what a day." Jim's voice was wistful.

A group of large, round buildings came into view. A road sign read: FISHING WORLD, NEXT EXIT. The Electrabus turned, proceeding to a large gate. As Jim and Bill got off the bus and onto a solar-powered shuttle cart, they stared at five buildings, which resembled oil-storage

63

tanks of the Nineties. Constructed of metal and windowless, they were painted different shades of blue. The shuttle driver asked where they'd be fishing, nodding as each man answered. The shuttle cart stopped at a dark blue building. When Jim stepped down, both Bill and the driver said, "Good luck."

"Same to you. I'll bring the lunch and meet you at noon," said Jim. Inside the building, he walked along a dim curving corridor to a Plexiglas booth. Inside was a woman, who asked, "Deep-sea fishing?" Jim nodded and paid for his ticket. The woman said, "Good luck. Just follow the corridor."

The curving hall ended at a door, which opened as he approached. Inside scenic ocean videos played on a curved wall of a huge round room, where a dolphin leaped, a gull swooped and a shark fin looked ominous. Muted diesel boat engines growled. Ten fighting chairs sat in a large semi-circle. In front of each chair was a replica of a yacht's stern rail. There was the smell of ocean breezes and Jim thought he tasted salt on his lips.

A tanned young man...dressed in shorts, boat shoes and billed cap ... said cheerfully, "Welcome aboard, Mr. Harding. I'm Jonathon, the first mate. Ready to go fishing?"

"I guess so," answered Jim. "How does this work, anyway?"

Your tuna rod is heavy-duty, the reel is an 80 wide two speed Penn, the line is hundred-pound test and the lure we're trolling is a Mexican Flag. Any questions?" asked the mate. "I only know what I read in the brochures. I'm not sure that I'll know what to do," said Jim. His uneasiness grew.

"Don't worry, I'll talk you through, no sweat. Here's your lucky fishing hat."

Jim donned the black, virtual-scene helmet and adjusted the audio. Now the wall video projections were obscured, he saw only the colorful, feathered lure skipping in the boat's wake. He relaxed. The fighting chair was as comfortable as his aero-recliner at home. Suddenly, the distinctive, harsh buzz of line pulling against drag, drilled into Jim's head.

"Hookup!" Jonathan yelled.

Boat engines slowed. Someone put the rod into his hands. His arm and shoulder muscles tensed against the heavy pull of a big fish. He braced his legs against the foot rests. "Atta boy, Jim," said Jonathan.

Inside the helmet, Jim saw a huge Blue Marlin leap out of the water, shake its enormous head, slash its bill at empty air, and struggle to break free. Jim could feel its power and grunted, trying to conserve his strength. Two hours later, he was gaining only a few inches of line with each renewed effort but felt that the marlin was tiring.

"Color," called Jonathan, leaning over the stern and staring down into the water, "we got color, here." The mate could see the fish.

Only then, when the fish's weight was suddenly gone, did Jim remember. This wasn't real but only an illusion. The reality of what was and what was not, broke the bubble of his exhilaration. Though his heart pounded and he was breathing hard, disappointment washed over him.

Jim removed the helmet. tipped Jonathan and walked out, not stopping at the trophy room which sold small marlin replicas. Later, Jim waited on a bench outside the building, where Bill was salmon fishing . Memories, of how things once were, flooded his mind.

When the scientists warned us about global warming, we paid no attention. Like fools, we kept using spray cans and air-conditioners. We clear-cut forests and burned wood and fossil fuels until the air turned yellow. Our eyes stung--our throats were raw. El Ninós came oftener with droughts and floods. Lakes grew stagnant , rivers ran brown. Fish died, but it didn't stop us. Instead, we built manufacturing plants in countries with no pollution controls. Now, fish and animal species are disappearing, gone forever, while we play these childish games. God help us all.

When Bill came out, his head drooped and his shoulders sagged, "How was the salmon fishing?" Jim asked.

Bill held up his trophy, one small package of imitation smoked salmon, and said, "I'm through fishing, Jim. It's just too sad."

Winter birds tapping
throughout snow covered yard
Morse code messages.

La Vonne Schoneman

the last whooping cranes
sit and silently stare
all fifty of them

Leonardo Alishan

LETTING GO

The tired, unsteady beat
of my heart struggles
against the swelling tide
of fluid build-up
within my lungs and limbs.
I fear the steps I must take.
As I stand on the shore
Of the Jordan River.
I am alone except for one
Whose hand of love is holding mine,
Not ready to let me go.
I am compelled to wade into the cold waters
As I struggle to breathe.
The hand of love continues to hold
And I look back and plead
"Come with me."
The long day has darkened into night.
I feel the rolling waves
Attempting to drown my love
Until I hear these words,
"Honey, how much longer can you go on?"
With only fingers touching now
My head submerged in calmer water
In the river's depth I am
Immersed in a much stronger light.
I hear the parting words of my love,
"Honey, God's arms are open wide
Walk right in!"
"Precious Lord, take my hand."
I am compelled to wade into the cold waters
As I struggle to breathe.
The hand of love continues to hold
And I look back and plead,
"Come with me."
The long day has darkened into night,

I feel the rolling waves
Attempting to drown my love
Until I hear these words,
"Honey, how much longer can you go on?"
With only fingers touching now
My head submerged in calmer water
In the river's depth I am
Immersed in a much stronger light,
I hear the parting words of my love,
"Honey, God's arms are open wide
Walk right in!"

Frances Darby

catching a dull flash
from the darkening window
his metal snuff can

Pat Laster

From: *Muse of Fire*

park walking trail
solitude--except for
the butterflies

Pat Laster

From: *Frogpond*

THIS IS NOT A POEM ABOUT A TREE

> Love this, not man apart from this…
> Robinson Jeffers

The great poetry guru said:
No more poems on nature,
nature has been done to death.
Chose another subject.
Give me one more recitation
on the redness of roses
and I'll scream!
No more tributes to trees,
no lyrics to leaves,
unless you are a latter-day
Keats, Shelley or Shakespeare,
no more ballades on birds.
Write about man, only man.
When the great poetry guru writes,
what is his great subject ...
    man the isolated,
    man the self-loving,
    man the destructive,
    man the uncomprehending?
When the great poetry guru walks past a rose,
a tree, a blade of grass, the dew on the rose,
the acorn in the tree, the beetle on the blade
of grass shining black; when he sees any bird,
    does he see life or death or both?
Does the great poetry guru understand that without roses
    without trees,
    without birds,
    his life, any life
    is unnatural and decreased?

Barbara Brent Bower

ALWAYS PAINT A WHITE HORSE

Paint the shadows on a white horse...
pastel dawn is perfect for unicorns
hazy cornflower or lilac...
a match for yellow-haired virgins
trying to catch one.

Pegasus has to be painted
on a cloud-soaked day when
billowy cirrus and nimbus
play games with a sea-blue sky--
use lace and feathers to explain the dream.
It is always a white horse...
like the one George rode
when he slew the dragon...
the stallion that whisked Richard
away to the Crusades...
the steed that carried Lancelot
to his Guinevere.

Work softly when you paint
a real horse—
unless you want him to ride off
the page into a crimson legend
you never meant to paint.

Frances Brinkley Cowden
From: *Of Butterflies and Unicorns*

YOUNG WRITERS

AUTOBIOGRAPHY OF AN ELEVEN YEAR OLD

Athena Charlotte Fuzzy, Etc.
Wacky, humorous, sensitive, unique
Daughter of Kathleen, cousin of Annie
Lover of sweets, goof-off time, and learning.
Who feels that the world should stop at times, that people should be
able to use all of their brain power, and
that everyone should be able to fly.
Who needs time to do nothing, people to confide in, and dreams.
Who fears cockroaches, the Locker Room, and the moment before I die.
Who gives an enthusiastic effort, a long-lasting friendship, and a bite of
my own chocolate cake.
Who would like to see Europe, people flying, and good dreams come true.
Resident of the Western Hemisphere
Rachel

Rachel White

WIND

Moving.
Playfully running.
Whispering in my ear.
Disturbing the leaves.
Cool and fresh.
Wind.
Wild and shrieking.
Overpowering.
Exhilarating and terrifying.
Destroying.
Wet and warm.
Wind.
Icy and driving.
Cold with snow.
Blinding.
Wild yet silent.
Wind.
A playful beast.
A spoiled child.
Kind when happy.
Devil when riled.

Eric Rogers

IN THE SKY

I would like to fly,
In the dark dark sky at night,
I would like to fly.

Angelica DePrimo

THAT DAY

I went to school as normal, that day,
I talked with my friends under the sun's warmest ray.
I laughed and I ate in the cafeteria that day,
never knowing what was happening a thousand miles away.

Far away, but not far enough,
some boys decided that they'd had enough -
Before the day was over, innocent blood was spilled,
The lives of fifteen people had suddenly been stilled.

Because respect was not demanded,
because those boys weren't reprimanded.
For those now dead,
more tears are shed.

They said they were teased when they didn't fit the trend,
so they caused fifteen lives to draw to an end.
But they had on their own chosen to wear black,
so there was no reason for any attack.

Now everyone gathers in circles, join hands,
now everyone gathers all over the lands.
For fifteen lost souls who had yet to live life,
all that's left for their families is misery and strife.

No one would have thought,
If those boys had been taught.
They wouldn't have had the intent,
To bring about this tragic event.
But now it's too late, At any rate.
For those fifteen now dead, so many still bow their heads.

Sarah Gosline

IN TRANSIT

A man sees a woman on a train.
The doors are sealed, the seats are limited.
Reluctantly he squeezes himself past
her thick body to the window seat.
Why did she sit on the aisle? he thinks,
To make things inconvenient for him?
Everyone is always working for themselves,
he thinks, no one ever thinks of me.
Of what use is the window seat to me? he thinks.
The train moves so fast his eyes
can't focus on anything outside.
The man stares out the window-
sees meaningless color zip past him.
Over time it hypnotizes him.
He forgets the concerns of his work,
the city he is racing away from.
Meaningless colors allow him
meaningless thoughts.
The man sighs.
The woman in the seat beside him
leans over the armrest to say
in a voice too loud that she
always remembers how much
her son loved the window seat on a train
when he was little. She says
she loves to watch people letting
the speeding colors steal their concerns.
 She says she's never met a person yet
who wouldn't kill to get a window seat.

Carolyn Moir

WE

We rise each morning with the sun,
  or before the sun, depending on the season.
We pull on trendy outfits
  as we rub the sleep from our eyes.
We fill our bellies with popular,
  celebrity-endorsed cereal,
  and head off to school.
We are concussed to maneuver
  Arabic symbols into bumpy lines
  to add and subtract,
  multiply and divide.
We combine series
  of lines and circles,
  curves and squigglies,
  only to produce a stupid story
  about an old man and a stubborn fish.
We pull out our little brown sacks
  filled with fattening snack foods
  and lunchmeat
  then spread nasty rumors about our best friends
  without thinking twice.
We have more obsolete statistics
  jammed into our brains
  about zygotes and kanji and playwrights.
We return to our homes,
  only to continue under this blind manipulation
  for hours,
  writing papers and memorizing facts,
  missing Dawsons Creek and Friends,
  and the Simpsons.
We fall asleep
  long after darkness has fallen, but then
We rise in the morning with the sun.

Carly Kiel

FORGOTTEN

Stripped of their beauty and strength
Lying naked and vulnerable
Are the once stoic mountains of Canada

Hiding in rural areas
Chiseled with highways
And ancient train tracks
Are the secluded mountains of Canada

Wind beaten
And drained
Eroded
And haggard
Are the exhausted mountains of Canada

Overlooked
And neglected
Forgotten
And erased
Are the raped mountains of Canada

Radha Gajjar

TOMORROW

It's somewhere,
off in the distance.
Peaking around the corner, always teasing.
Somehow untouchable.
Exciting and mysterious, foreboding and
captivating.
No one knows what it will hold,
No one can tell if there will always be one.
Something we take for granted.
God will provide us with a tomorrow.

Jennifer Leigh Wheeler

"Kissena Park, Queens, New York," by Najwa Salam Brax

"Alabama Scene," Sue Mobley

Grandmother Earth

Salutes

ALABAMA POETS AND WRITERS

"Our Alma Mater," Jack Daniel
reprinted from *Cherokee Alabama*

YOU ARE MY THOUGHTS

This morning you are my thoughts
And I am persuaded,
By the strident, singing call of
Sunday southbound geese
And by the acrid, nasal taste of
Close-by burning leaves
To tell you this...

That sounds and smells of
Autumns past and autumn now
Shall always speak of you.

That frost-dipped fingers
Years and miles away from here
Will paint your face.

That leaves in gentle stirrings
Shall ever speak your voice
And bid me peace.

Precious is the time we shared
And all we learned,
And how we cared.

Esther O'Donald

FIELD WORKERS SINGING

Not so high yet as to be hot,
The sun calls the pickers to the field;
Still not committed to the work ahead,
Most move in solemn file like drones, while others
With youthful energy, resist the mood--
Dampening of the low-key morning air.
The recurring sway and dip as they
Pick the peas has not yet become a rhythm;
Muscles still stiff from the long yesterday
Spent tediously hovering over the vines,
Will slowly warm and stretch to efficiency,
Cautiously letting go their reluctance.
Patiently, with practice, singles become crew,
Laboring in tandem at what they do best.
A worker is heard to say that he feels like
Part of a locust swarm, engorging the crop.
Such membership is bred of long sharing of
The common bond of daily survival.
The sun, blooming in power overhead,
Starts taking its toll of the laboring pace.
Across the field the crews are beginning
To feel the drag of heat and monotony.
As if by signal a solitary voice
Is heard, like a small bird lifting with the wind.
With almost churchly reverence the song
Sends out small threads seeking to reweave
The slacking pattern of performance.
Slowly, one by one, the enjoining notes
Become a chorus, lifting the pickers
From the ordinary dust of their day.

Madge Pfleger

A CAT NAMED POEM OR IS IT A POEM NAMED CAT?

A poem lies asleep in my mind
like a cat curled before a hearth.

How can I coax her out?

Lacking a saucer of cream
and at arm's length,
I stroke her gently:
softly scratch her chin.

Poem awakes - moves one step away -
then stretches, arching her back:
forefeet extended, claws in carpet,
hips higher than head,
tail straight as a steeple.

She lolls looping tail around toes,
and, using a bit of pink sandpaper,
licks her paws.
She curls one up, washes her face.
Grooming complete, she sits serenely.
I inch closer, thinking, "Gotcha!"
But, in that instant,
Poem, emerald eyes glowing inscrutably,
exits, aloof as an Egyptian queen.

Bettye Kramer Cannizzo

SEA, STONE, DREAMS
(VENICE)

The sun, linked like a gold chain on the waves,
draws me back to my childhood days
when white sand beaches warmed my toes,
and sandcastles drew me into dreams.

And now, plowing through
the Grand Canal, as the gold sun-links float
on the dark water and reflect
off the palace windows, I feel
transposed to another time--when fish,
silks and satins, gold and silver,
or pearls were bartered for money,
women, or food. The ghosts
of those long dead, float with me, flood me,
women wearing veils and sandals,
next to others in brocaded dresses
and masked faces. Brightly colored
ribbons drape the gondolas
and beads of Venetian glass drape noble lords
and courtesans alike.

When the bells of St. Mark's
ring the noon hour, echoed by a hundred others,
I climb the inside stairs,
push back the pigeons
on the balcony behind the golden horses,
and stare down on the tourists that crowd the square.
I feel at home looking out into the bay,

the water a sparkling blue
as a sail boat glides by.

I touch the roughness of the stone,
feel the pulse of poets and artists long dead,
and see the stains of word-marred walls.

I see the white sand beach of an outer island,
and see myself as a child
when the sea took my sand castles, my dreams.
And I pray the sea--that is so much a part here--
does not take this dream away.

Mary E. Halliburton

THE CANDY TREE

In nineteen thirty-seven, I was ten.
Starvation stalked the land, depression held
the world in gaunt and hungry hand.

Why then do I remember
with a joy never felt before or since
a Christmas, warm and sweet and bright,
filled with light, and the taste
of chocolate?

It was the tree,
the candy tree my mother
made for me, of Butterfingers, Baby Ruths,
Hershey's Kisses we called Silver Bells,
tiny peppermint candy canes,
red and white, penny candies all,
little squares of fudge
wrapped in cellophane,
tied with string and hung
on branches of a scrawny pine
cut from a sedge-field.

Unforgettable candy tree
to delight the eyes, the heart
of any child, but for a hungry child
who'd never seen or dared to hope
for chocolate riches such as these,
it was a Christmas-lighted
dream.

A candy tree, one day of paradise
in era gray with want and need and faded
clothes. A memory now
warm as tears, bright as Christmas lights,
it tastes of peppermint candy canes
and chocolate.

Reese Danley-Kilgo

Photograph by Jane E. Allen

HOMELESS
(After Hurricane Opal)

The LUSTFUL EYE surveyed the countryside
    with its disastrous intentions
        and then
The MALICIOUS MOUTH spewed out its venom
    of wild, raging winds.
The foundation shook with a powerful vengeance
    and then fell with a crackling eruption,
        its insides exposed to the RAW TONGUES of
    nature.

A dwelling place was destroyed that night--the
    occupants scattering asunder,
        lost in the black cloak of midnight
     fury

          HOMELESS,
      their sweet honeycombs still
        clinging to the side
           of the fallen oak tree.

Jane E. Allen

"Gate on the DePriest Farm." Otis Henderson

"Eastern Box Turtle," Neal Hogenbirk

TURTLE

You, little Atlas, walking stone,
rustle your way through summer's

tattle; baffled, cast your marigold
eye on marvels; what was oak, leaf-loam, laurel

roars, a blacktop road. Stop. Wait up.
Dogflies and deerflies know what softness

pulses at the core. We go earth-deep
and sleeping puts us wise. You, fossil, you

keep on your carapace, your hinged plastron.
Cricket-picker, you are always home.

Coyotes might balk your brave straddle, or
a rusted truck skidding the blind curve

below these yaupon hollies slap
you clean over into mottled, tesellated bone.

Behold: I scoop you up and set you,
marching, down beneath crepe myrtles. Shun

macadam, will you? You're Triassic. I ask this:
Outlast curbs, fences, me, and traffic.

Jeannette Barnes

SHORT CHILDHOOD

Your childhood's past.
It went too fast.
How could I know
How fast you'd grow?
Time will not wait
Or hesitate.
I watch confused.
The present moved.

Faye Gaston

AN AUTUMN HIGH

In my fall garden
globes of garlic lean
crazily over the strawberry bed inebriated
with the sweetness of earth.
Do they remember
their lavender visitor: the tiny butterfly identical
in color to their flowered heads?
Do they hear the Canada geese
honking overhead,
veeing to feeding fields?
Do they see my sheets
flapping under an October-blue sky?
By some mysterious intuition,
can the garlic discern
that I, too, am intoxicated
with the sweetness of earth?

Bettye Krammer Cannizzo

"Earth Treasures," Judith Baker Jones

HURRAH, HURRAH

Susan Murphy

After the rain, ant mounds rise out of the Alabama soil like welts on the landscape, hives in every sense of the word. Hundreds of them, thousands of them. And every mouthful of every mound is carried to the surface by an individual ant. I recently read that, in the Amazon rainforest, ants cover roughly four times more area than all the local vertebrate animals combined. Judging from the number of ant hills in my neighborhood alone, I'd say that the Alabama ant population couldn't be far behind. Sometimes, it seems like my subdivision is just one giant anthill with a few houses perched on top for color.

Last year, however, when the weather was so hot and beastly, one ant colony decided to break the concrete ceiling and spend the summer inside my house. They began by sending in a couple of little ant scouts, who were, from all appearances, just six-legged tourists out to see the sights. These guys seemed harmless enough, walking around in circles and bumping into each other, so I let them pass. But, behind those dazed looks and wobbly antennae lurked the very heart of ant colony reconnaissance. Their mission? Find an interior route that could handle three or four lanes of traffic, and determine which household locations offered bed and breakfast. After a few minutes of casual whistling and shuffling, the ant scouts made a beeline back to the colony to file their report. My house must have received a five star rating, because less than an hour later, hundreds of their brother (sister?) ants began streaming into the kitchen.

At first, I tried to reason with the little guys. Being a live-and-let live kind of person, I hate to just haul out the Raid unless it's absolutely necessary. Besides, I kind of like ants. They're industrious little creatures, even if they are a bit misguided, and with the work ethic being what it is today, I hate to discourage good honest labor in any form.

Ants are also entertaining in a low-level sort of way. Watching them go about their daily rounds may not be "Deep Impact" or "General Hospital," but on a hot summer day, it's all the excuse I need not to go back inside and fold the laundry. However, after several minutes of sweeping away the new arrivals, it became apparent that this ant colony was trying to save me the trouble of coming outside to watch them by bringing all of their troops indoors.

For the next few days, I tried to solve the ant invasion problem by making my house as ant unfriendly as possible. I caulked the windows and kept the counters cleared of soda cans. I put the bread in the oven and the cookie jar in the refrigerator. I scrubbed and sealed until there wasn't a single area in my house that would indicate we were open to ant colonization.

But, these ants were a particularly incorrigible crowd. They started coming up through the floor vents, climbing through the electrical outlets and moseying into my microwave oven via ... well, I never did figure out how they managed that. And I don't know if you've noticed this, but ants are not a particularly sentimental bunch. When one line of troops is taken out with a dish towel or sink sprayer, another group immediately takes its place, marching right over the bodies of their fallen comrades. After exhausting an entire roll of paper towels and every other non-violent avenue I could think of, I was forced to haul out my secret weapon - the vacuum cleaner. For lack of a better plan, five hundred ants got a one way trip to the basement vacuum system receptacle. But the ants kept coming.

Finally, partly from curiosity and partly because my vacuum cleaner was overheating, I decided to sit down and just watch the ants for a while. With the threat of turbo-transportation lifted, small groups of ants once again began cautiously moving across the countertop. Two minutes later, great *columns* of ants came marching across my kitchen floor. They were focused. They were organized. They were relentless.

Past juice spills and overlooked potato chips they continued. Where in the world were they headed? To my potted plants, bless their little ant hearts. It was sheer brilliance. The pots of ivy and African violets offered the ants all the comforts of a rich soil home in a controlled climate. Adventure, air conditioning, and cable TV. They were like miniature ant RVs.

Being a former teacher, I had to give the ants points for creative problem solving, but I couldn't let them stay. Call me a fuddy duddy, but I really didn't want 5,000 ants summering in my kitchen. Somehow, I had to get rid of them before they collectively figured out how to open the refrigerator and operate the remote control.

I remembered reading that no one ever really eradicates ant colonies. They just convince them to move. So, wearing rubber gloves against the stings and arrows of the occupying ant troops, I carried all of my potted plants onto the screened-in porch where the weather was a crisp 105 degrees. By the next morning, the ants had been convinced to seek out greener and cooler pastures.

We've had another warm spell lately, with very little rain. Yesterday, I spotted a couple of ants in the bathroom, just kind of wandering around. Well, this time I'm not buying it. I don't care how thirsty they get, they can't move into my shower stall. I'll never be able to haul that thing outdoors. So, this time, along with cleaning off the counters and sealing up the toothpaste, I put a can of Raid right out in plain view.

You've got to ask yourself, little ant scouts, do you feel lucky?

CHRISTMAS CHRYSALIS

Rebecca Davis Henderson

My pruning shears paused in mid-bite. There on the rose of Sharon was a big, beautiful cocoon. What a lovely gift; a meaningful symbol for this season of hope.

Advent is not always so warm, and soon the cold dark days, more typical of winter, followed Christmas. There were times when it seemed spring would never come, but finally March brought the brightness of daffodils, and April brought green leaves. The cocoon brought nothing.

For weeks I checked the bush every day, then discouraged, I'd ignore it. Could it be dead? Searching for a clue, I hoped the fibers at the end had separated a little, but no, nothing had changed.

Twilight was falling one day in the middle of May as I trudged up the driveway. My daily walk had drained me and for some reason I stopped there.

All the months of disappointment faded as I knelt at the bush. On a limb near the cocoon, with wings opened flat, as if waiting for something, was what I had been waiting for. Quickly I rushed into the house for a camera. With darkness descending, it was impossible to focus properly, but the flash recorded the moment.

My long vigil rewarded, elated and satisfied, I said, "Goodnight," to the beautiful visitor.

The next morning found my winged friend still there. Neighbors came over to admire and we expected any moment it would take wing.

Saturday is a busy chore day, but several times I checked the bush. This was puzzling. Why doesn't it fly away, I wondered.

Sunday morning found me up early to let the dog out. With sleep not long from my half-focused eyes, my bare feet wandered over to the bush. As in a dream, too wonderful to be true, I gazed in disbelief.

Perfect mirror images were they, as I stood on holy ground. Creeping closer, I could see that "my" moth was the one with the fat round body, and her visitor had a long slender body.

She had been waiting, receptive and her prince had come. He had been active, searching and he found her. The ancient energies of opposites were fully expressed in this sacred moment of wholeness.

Days later, I brought the simple gray symbol into the house.

> An empty cocoon now on the shelf
> A memory is all that is left

But that memory is still vivid almost a year later as Holy Week unfolds. The splendor of an exuberant creator majestically pulls out all the stops, by frosting the orchards with pink and tossing blossoms like confetti, yellow and lavender, across the landscape. And when the dogwood burst forth like an anthem, my heart will sing the psalms.

The sight of the cocoon continues to remind me:

> An empty tomb beside the sea
> And hope was born for you and me ...

Now this same joyful hope has put straw in my new birdhouse. Long ago, it is said, straw filled another's tiny bed.

The earth is ready.

WARTIME HOLIDAY

Auguste Black

The No. 5 trolley from Ensley was almost empty. Only three passengers were huddled on the cold wooden benches, their winter coats pulled tightly around them. Midge stepped aboard and gave the conductor her money.

She stood for a moment at the front of the car. The small heater by the conductor's seat was a spot of warmth after the brisk chill of waiting alone at the trolley stop. In 1943 few people rode a trolley at seven o'clock on Christmas morning. The country was at war and most of the young men were away. Those who remained worked long hours and were glad for a day of rest.

Midge had been asked to work. Holidays paid double time and sixty cents an hour was more than her father made in the steel mills and her family needed the money.

As she sat in the streetcar, she looked at the other passengers. Behind the "Colored" sign toward the back of the bus sat two middle-aged black women. From their laughter and loud talking, Midge realized they were friends, each going to work for their white families.

The only other passenger was a sailor. When she looked up at him, he smiled and said, "Merry Christmas!" As she returned the smile and greeting, he jumped up from his seat.

"May I sit with you? No one should ride alone on Christmas."

She shrugged her shoulders and nodded. Her shyness made it hard for her to talk to a strange man, but it was Christmas and he was a serviceman.

Approaching her seat, he removed his sailor cap and with a grand flourish, he put it over his heart. "Hi, I'm Seaman Robert Harrison. 'Curly' to my friends." His blue eyes twinkled as he replaced his cap on his new crew cut and shook her hand. Midge laughed. He sat down beside her and asked, "What are you doing on a streetcar so early on Christmas Day?"

"I'm going to church and then to work. What are you doing on a streetcar so early on Christmas Day?"

The sailor laughed. "I'm on my way home for Christmas. My family doesn't know I'm coming. I just finished boot camp and I'm due to be sent out after New Year's. I have to be back on base at midnight. I'm in the Seabees."

Seaman Robert Harrison was eager to talk and Midge was a good listener. They were busy talking when the conductor called out, "Downtown," to remind them of the end of the line. Everyone disembarked. They all nodded and repeated, "Merry Christmas!" Then Midge and the sailor went their separate ways.

When the store opened, Midge was at her counter in the tobacco and candy section near the entrance of the drug store. Only she and the pharmacist were working this Christmas Day. A few customers came in before lunch time, mostly for cigarettes and boxes of candy for last minute gifts. The morning passed slowly.

With nothing to do, Midge's thoughts returned to the sailor on the bus. He reminded her of a young puppy. He was so proud of being in the Navy and so excited about going home. I wonder if he has a girlfriend, she thought.

By eleven o'clock Midge was bored and feeling sorry for herself. She finally took out her sandwich and her thermos of tea. As she ate, she looked through several magazines out for sale. Nothing was very interesting. She thought of all the people in their homes enjoying themselves.

The afternoon went slower than the morning. At two, Midge bought a candy bar and nibbled at it slowly, trying to kill time. Her thoughts went again to the young sailor. He was lucky to be going home. This second

Christmas of the war found many families with missing loved ones.

Three o'clock came and went. At 4:45 Midge began covering the merchandise. "I'm leaving on the dot of five or I'll miss my trolley. I don't want to wait on the deserted corner an hour for the next one."

Suddenly the door opened. Standing at the counter, gasping for air, was the sailor. "I was afraid I couldn't get here before you closed. Please, can you wrap a box of candy for my girlfriend? I'm meeting her in a half hour. Please!"

He picked a small box of the best candy. She wrapped it as he searched through the cards. As she finished wrapping, he paid for the card and candy. With a wave and a "Merry Christmas," he left.

Looking at the clock, Midge saw it was five after five. "I've missed my streetcar." Tears came to her eyes and the extra money she had made could not bring any Christmas spirit to her heart. She locked up the register and handed the key to the pharmacist.

Outside, the street was empty and the air was cold. Two blocks away, she saw her trolley turning the corner. It would make no difference if she rushed now. Pulling her scarf over her chin, she lowered her head against the wind coming off the tall buildings.

Suddenly someone touched her elbow. "If you hurry, we can catch the car as it makes its loop around downtown."

Looking up, she recognized the sailor. He grabbed her hand and they started running the three blocks to where the streetcar turned again to leave town. As the conductor waited for them, they climbed aboard, out of breath and unable to speak. They were the only passengers. Midge sat down and the sailor sat beside her. As soon as he could speak, he handed her the box of candy and the card she had wrapped earlier. Smiling, he whispered, "Merry

Christmas!" She opened the card and read, "For the beginning of a wonderful friendship."

Suddenly the street was filled with Christmas music.

"Depot at Cherokee, Alabama (1940)," Jack Daniel

ANGELS: MESSENGERS OF LOVE AND GRACE
Edited by Frances Brinkley Cowden (Life Press)
ISBN 1-88429-18-5
Review by Malra Treece

Twenty-four essays describing true-life experiences of fifteen writers are included in this attractively presented volume.
It is illustrated throughout by drawings prepared by Editor Cowden's 7-and 8-year old grandchildren.
One of the few poems, as written by Russell H. Strauss, expresses the theme of the book:

SUNSET

God's chimneys flicker,
Stars and guardian angels
Report for night shift

The angels described in the essays, however, do wait for nightfall, but appear whenever or wherever they are needed. All the writers are convinced, or nearly so, that they have been saved or comforted by angels, some disguised as good Samaritans that disappear when their miracles are accomplished.

For example, Frances Cowden describes how her son was discovered after an almost fatal accident in Arkansas. A truck driver ministered to him, called an ambulance, telephoned his parents with specific directions to the hospital. The trucker, or angel, did not identify himself and was never heard from again. Frances writes:
"Was he an angel or a very good Samaritan? Does it really make any difference?"

Gayle Husley describes how she was saved from almost certain death by huge unseen wings that floated her car to safety from a pile-up on an interstate. Frances Darby tells a similar story of her automobile floating in space so that she was saved from an accident.

Louise Hays describes two encounters with an angel in hospital rooms. She ends her essay, however, with these words: "I never saw her again, leaving me to wonder if she was real or if I had given her wings made from my gossamer hold on reality."

Mattie Abbott describes how an angel in a pink dress floated beside the window of a truck that carried the young Mattie away from her rural home to a nursing school in Memphis.

Editor Cowden writes: "This book could raise more questions than it answers. Do angels sometimes defy laws of nature? Do they save us in supernatural ways because we have not yet fulfilled God's plan for us?" Even the most skeptical readers will be intrigued by this interesting and convincing book.

****

Thoroughbreds of Railroading: Yesterday and Today,
ISBN 1-884289-26-6
By Jack McDaniel
Grandmother Earth, 1999, 312 pages, 8 1/2x 11,
Review by Frances Darby

Jack Daniel's latest book is a pictorial album (378 photographs) depicting the locomotives and railroad people who have kept the trains running from the turn of the century until the present day. The emphasis is on the last half of the century. It features the Southern Railway System and the Norfolk Southern Corporation from Memphis to Chattanooga, Tennessee, and Sheffield to Birmingham, Alabama.

In addition to the photographs, documents range from old operations memos to seniority list as late as 1998. Daniel explains, "Railroading is a grand, noisy spectacle, and we tend to emphasize action, inevitably overlooking some gentler traditions." Every railroad collector will want a copy of this piece of railroad history, which may be obtained from the author or from the publisher at P. O. Box 241986, Memphis, TN 38124.

FROM THE JUDGES

JUDGING THE POEMS

Clovita Rice

    I enjoyed reading the poems! You have many good strong entries. It wasn't too difficult to select the top ten in each category, but after that the judging became difficult, for these poets know how to develop imagery, how to appeal to the senses, how to return the reader with them into some nostalgic experience, and sometimes to nudge the reader toward something told so beautifully and memorably that the reader can't forget it, wants to read it again and again.
    The two first place winners will linger with me. "Field Workers Singing" is a painting which you can see coming alive with movement and with song, leaving us with the reminder that music can change the ordinary dust of the day. "Wolf-Wind" is a poem that will haunt me. An aged Indian man is reminiscing about meeting his young wife, their eating "thicket plums by full moonlight," recalling the sweetness and wonder of their early lives but now facing her illness, with his promise that should she die tonight he will follow soon. Though the themes are not new, the poems are both new approaches and beg the reader to focus in closely and feel the moods of each poem.

■■■

JUDGING THE HAIKU CONTEST

Pat Laster

    As you know, each poet—be it contest entrant or judge—comes to his or her writing from personal experiences.
    My experience with haiku—my preferences, my basis for judging—comes from being published—and rejected—in such journals as *Frogpond, Modern Haiku, Point Judith Light, Piedmont Literary Review*, and the newsletter-formatted *Haiku Headlines* and *Muse of Fire*. My choices of winners reflect the

learning gained from the editors of the above-mentioned presses during the last several years.

Forty-nine poems were culled on the first reading for a variety of reasons.
- Eleven were not haiku, but senryu.
- Fifteen contained titles, a traditional no-no. Senryu are sometimes titled except in major journals where they are grouped together under the Senryu heading.

The poetic devises so useful in other poetry—similes, metaphors and personification—are NOT ACCEPTABLE in the best haiku tradition, despite a *ByLine* haiku judge's preferences. One poem in this contest contained both a simile and a metaphor Don't attribute personal qualities to nature. Truth must be served.
- Watch for redundancies. "Supplication" and "heavenward" in the same poem is a waste of syllables.
- Present tense is usually a requisite in moments of wonder or delight.
- Some poems need revising to make them more musical. Others need a change in the way they're lined up/out.
- Do not be bound by the 5-7-5 syllable straitjacket (how's that for a metaphor?)

Twenty two poems went through a second reading, indicating they had possibilities. Some lacked the musical quality necessary, usually because of the stretch for 17 syllables. Descriptive words (adjectives) are a commentary of sorts and commentary is verboten. Poets show the images; the readers provide their own spin, vision. The predominant typography of haiku in the best journals uses very few or no caps or punctuation; each line completes a phrase/thought. Occasionally, a dash at the end of a line will help separate the two images. Otherwise we might conclude, as in one poem, that tulips were back from their trip. However, if a line can turn and become part of either of the other two, that is a plus.

The final eight poems were very competitive. They all contained the acceptable form: 1): a one-line image followed by two related lines, or vice versa; 2) a continuous phrase—usually not a complete sentence, though sometimes it is; 3) not constrained in the 5-7-5 syllabic pattern. No journal uses that anymore, only some state poetry society contests do. I wonder at the great discrepancy between journal haiku and contest haiku. Do you see a solution? A narrowing of the gap between them?

NOTES FROM SOME OF THE OTHER JUDGES

PROSE JUDGE

"I was honored to judge the prose for *Grandmother Earth 2000*. Making the final decisions was difficult, and I congratulate the winners!" **Florence Bruce**, Memphis, Tennessee, Editor of Writers on the River is a retired medical transcriptionist from Methodist Hospital and now works part-time at Baptist Hospital. She has won numerous awards including first place in Grandmother Earth's 1998 Prose Awards. She is an active member of the Lewis Center Chorus. In the current work-a-day world, she writes and edits with and for local physicians. She dabbles in poetry and fiction, and is a member of several writers' groups, including the Memphis Storytellers' League and the Poetry Society of Tennessee.

HUMOROUS POETRY

Michael Denington says, "I began writing poetry after retiring from an Air Force career about 12 years ago. I enjoy reading and writing both formal and free verse, and have been blessed with success in both types in contests and publications. My bedside table is loaded with poetry volumes, and I read poetry every day. Advice to contestants: a poem must have a message; always stay within the maximum number of lines specified; make sure your poem complies with any form specified; avoid contrived rhymes; imagery, imagery, imagery; and be realistic about entering poems in contests where they will have a chance. For example, a 12-line poem almost certainly will not do well in a contest allowing a maximum of 40 lines.

HUMOROUS PROSE

Louise Gearin is a published writer who has won awards in numerous contests. She said, "I find judging contests interesting. Some writing is obviously that of a beginner, but perhaps a beginner with promise. I believe, aside from obvious talent, that winners are those who have learned the important basics of the craft of writing and have used it to perfect their work."

Editor's Choice selections are made by the editors of *Grandmother Earth*. Some of the other special awards were judged by a committee selected from the total editorial staff.

A Special Thanks to Editorial Assistants:

Frances Darby
Lorraine Smith
E. Marcelle Zarshenas

CONTRIBUTORS

Barbara Abbott, Memphis, Tennessee, took an early retirement from her career as an art and English teacher with Shelby County, Tennessee schools to pursue other interests which include cooking, pottery and poetry. She is a member of the boards of the Poetry Society of Tennessee the National League of American Pen Women, Chickasaw Branch.
Adams, Burlingame California, is a national prize-winner.
Kareem Al-Darahi, Nashville, Tennessee, and **Leonardo Alishan**, Salt Lake City, Utah, appear for the second time in *Grandmother Earth.*. Leonardo sent several extra entries, explaining that he just wanted to support a good cause. Thanks!
Patty Ashworth, Memphis, Tennessee, is author of *Poems for a Rainy Night II*.
Annetta Talbot Beauchamp, Helena, Arkansas, a member of Poet's Roundtable of Arkansas East Central Branch. She frequently wins regional and national awards for her writing.
Burnette Bolin Benedict, Knoxville, Tennessee, is author of *Kinship*, lyrical poetry set in Tennessee, a Grandmother Earth Chapbook award winner.
Najwa Salam Brax lives in New York state and has been in Grandmother Earth several times.
Barbara Brent Brower, Okemos, Michigan, has been published in many journals and anthologies including: *The Muse Strikes Back Anthology* published by Story Line Press, *Crazy Quilt, The Lyric, Great River Review, Ruby, Tirra-Lirra* (Australia), to name a few. She is currently on a book tour reading from the new anthology, *The Leap Years—Women Reflect on Change, Loss and Love*, published by Beacon Press.
Marilyn Califf is a photographer and artist from Memphis, Tennessee.
Marcia Camp, Little Rock, Arkansas, won the Sybil Nash Abrams Award in 1984. Her poetry and prose appear in both regional and national publications.
Maureen Cannon is almost 77 years old and has been writing verse for most of her life. Editors have nodded, among them those at *McCALL'S, LADIES HOME JOURNAL, GOOD HOUSEKEEPING, THE SATURDAY EVENING POST, THE CHRISTIAN SCIENCE MONITOR, THE NEW YORK TIMES,*

LYRIC, READER'S DIGEST, etc. "I give workshops, programs at women's clubs, nursing homes, in the school system locally and farther afield, and, often I'm honored to be asked to judge contests, especially light verse ones!"

Jane Davis Carpenter is from Denver, Colorado.

Martha Carpenter, Memphis, Tennessee, has published in Christian publications.

Hollis K. Cathey lives in the Ozarks with his wife, Maurine and four dogs. "I've been writing for six years and am still learning. I attend three to four conferences yearly, including Mid-South. My office walls are adorned with many contest wins and so far this year I've sold five short stories. Also, I'm currently working on the third manuscript of a historical Western series.

Arla Clemons, Las Crosse, Wisconsin, is a retired physical education teacher, now pursuing her writing carrer. She has been published in the *Wisconsin Poets' Calendar, Touchstone* and *Grandmother Earth.*

John Crawford, Professor of English Literature at Henderson State University, Arkedelphia, Arkansas, is also a noted pianist.

Frances Darby contributed to *Our Golden Thread,* and has poetry in all of the *Grandmother Earth* series. She is the widow of the late Rev. James W. Darby, a United Methodist minister.

Frieda Beasley Dorris, Memphis, Tennessee, is one of the orginators of the Dorsimbra poetry form. A past president of the Poetry Society of Tennessee, she has won numerous awards for her poetry.

Anne Marie Dyer, Kentucky Colonel, Clearwater, Florida, is a private dectective. She likes to ride horses and has a dog named Colonel. She is the niece of Cornelius Hogenbirk.

Winifred Hamrick Farrar is Poet Laureate of Mississippi, and is widely published. She is a member of the Mississippi Poetry Society, the Poetry Society of Tennessee, and the NLAPW, Chickasaw Branch.

Evelyn Foote, Memphis, Tennessee, is a member of Mid-South Writers Association and the Poetry Society of Tennessee. She has published in several Christian publications.

Alice Garrison is from West Plains, Missouri.

Dena R. Gorrell, Edmond, Oklahoma is a widely published writer who often wins national awards.

Edith Guy is a Memphis member of the Poetry Society of Tennessee and has appeared in several Grandmother Earth publications.

Richard Hancock, Millington, Tennessee has been an aircraft pilot, a news broadcaster, assembly line worker, box boy, writer, fire department alarm operator dispatcher, teacher, computer programmer, minister, and sky diver.

Sandra Hancock, Huntington, Tennessee, has published in several Haiku publications.

Ruth Peal Harrell, Memphis, Tennessee, has conducted workshops explaining Kenneth Beaudoin's eye-poems. Her publications include *Voices International*.

Betty Heidelberger, Lexa, Arkansas, has been published in several literary magazines and has won numerous awards. She is one of the organizers of the Arkansas Poetry Day activities. She is president of the East Central Branch of Poets Roundtable of Arkansas

Nina Salley Hepburn, Cordova, Tennessee, is a freelance writer and has won several regional awards

Verna Lee Hinegardner, Poet Laureate of Arkansas is a past president of the Arkansas Pioneer Branch of The National League of American Penwomen; Past President of Poets' Roundtable of Arkansas; President of Roundtable Poets of Hot Springs; served 12 years on the board of National Federation of State Poetry Societies and chaired two of their national conventions; member of Poets' Study Club, Poetry Society of America, International Poetry Society, and is listed in The International Directory of Distinguished Leadership. Hinegardner was inducted into the Arkansas Writers' Hall of Fame in 1991; won their Sibyl Nash Abrams Award in 1973, 1979 and 1991; received the Arkansas Award of Merit in 1976 and 1983; and is the author of nine books of poetry.

Victoria Hodge, Memphis, Tennessee, is middle school music teacher at Evangelical Christian School. Her poem, "Be Still and Know," appears on a mural she painted for Colonial Park United Methodist Church. She won a first place award which was published in Seasons of the South, Dr. R. Paul Caudill publisher.

Ann Hoffman, Ft. Smith, Arkansas, is a member of the Poets' Roundtable of Arkansas, Oklahoma Writer's Federation Incorporated, Arkansas Ridgewriters, and the Poetry Society of Tennessee. She and her husband are frequent contest winners.

Jerry won first place in poetry in *Grandmother Earth V*. Ann is an LPN and takes care of special needs adults.

Cornelius Hogenbirk, Waretown, New Jersey, is a retired sales engineer. His hobbies are photography, gardening, and writing. His work has been in every issue of *Grandmother Earth*, under the name of Neal Hogenbirk.

Elizabeth Howard, Crossville, Tennessee, is the author of *Anemones*, Grandmother Earth, 1998 which contains poetry that has been previously published in journals and anthologies. She is a frequent award-winner.

Gayle Hulsey, Memphis, Tennessee, was published in *Angels: Messengers of Love and Grace*.

Jennifer Jensen is an attorney in Memphis, Tennessee.

Judith Baker Jones, has a line of cards using her photographs of flowers. Though from Fairway, Kansas, she has ties to Tennessee which include a grandmother named Tennessee.

Pug Jones, Hot Springs, Arkansas, has been married 49 years, has three children and six grandchildren. She started writing in '83. Credits include: Regular columns, features and photography for 13 magazine and 15 newspapers (staff and freelance). Wrote portions of 3 books on boating. Currently writes one weekly humor column, one monthly magazine feature, a monthly feature newspaper column and freelance assignments. Photographer, member of Outdoor Writers of America and South Eastern Press Association. She was a speaker at AWC '99.

Lise Kelly, Memphis, Tennessee, is a free-lance writer and computer expert. He has been a big supporter of the Memphis Literacy Council.

Pat Laster's first published poem was a haiku. From Arkadelphia, Arkansas, she has been writing since 1984 and has published ***windfall persimmons***, a book of Oriental forms, and ***Connecting Our Houses***, a flip, perpetual calendar of haiku/senryu which she wrote with Dorothy McLaughlin, New Jersey. Her haiku, senryu, and sequences have been published in *Modern Haiku, Haiku Headlines, Point Judith Light, Muse of Fire, Frogpond* and *Piedmont Literary Review*.

Gloria Lee, Memphis, Tennessee, and **Janice Levy**, Merrit, New York, appear for the first time in *Grandmother Earth*.

Rita Lurrie is a free-lance writer and coordinator of a senior citizens writing group at East Senior Citizen Center, at Gaisman,

Memphis, Tennessee. She has a variety of publications including, *Our Golden Thread*, and *Penhaligon Page*, England.

Thomas McDaniel, is an attorney in Memphis, Tennessee. He has been President and Poet Laureate of the Poetry Society of Tennessee.

Martha McNatt, Humboldt, Tennessee, is a former teacher, and director of the Child Nutrition Program for Madison County Schools. She is the author of *Feeding the Flock*, a cookbook for church kitchens, published by Bethany House, and *A Heritage Revisited*, a commissioned work by First Christian Church, Jackson, Tennessee. Her work has appeared in each of the Grandmother Earth anthologies, in *Grandmother Earth's Healthy and Wise Cookbook*, and in Life Press's *Our Golden Thread*. Martha is president of the Jackson Circle Branch of the National League of American Pen Women.

Margot Marler, Rossville, Georgia, has had work in every issue of *Grandmother Earth*. She has sent copies of each issue to several libraries in her area.

Dodie Messer Meeks's poetry placed first in the Michigan State Poetry Society's 1999 awards and appears in several anthologies including *The Anthology of Magazine Verse* and *Yearbook of American Poetry*. Dodie Messer Meeks once covered Galveston for the *Houston Chronicle*. She would love to hear from other water colorists and/or poets through her web-page. Her e-mail is: Dodiemeeks@juno.com.

Kolette Montague is from Centerville, Utah.

Sherry Organ, Searcy, Arkansas is active in the Searcy Writers' Association.

June Owens, Zephyrhills, Florida, is 72 years old and has published many poems and won many prizes. Her first book of poetry, *Tree Line*, published by Prospect Press won the Sparrowgrass Poet of the Year Award.

Olga Warner Penizin, is from Waxhaw, North Carolina. **Ruth Rakestraw**, Springdale Arkansas, appear for the first time in *Grandmother Earth*.

Rosemary Stephens, Memphis, Tennessee, is a widely published author of prose, poetry, and fiction. Her novels were published by Scholastic Books, her stories by *Seventeen* and literary journals. She has won national awards and has appeared frequently in university quarterlies and anthologies. Her first collection of poems, *Eve's Navel* won a publication award from *South and*

West. She holds the Ph.D. in English from the University of Mississippi. She was first place winner of the Eve Braden Hatchett Tennessee Bicentennial Award given by Grandmother Earth III.
Patricia W. Smith, Memphis, Tennessee, is editor of the Grandmother Earth Series. The poem which appears in this collection is reprinted from Tennessee Voices. Past president of the Poetry Society of Tennessee, she is currently a director. She is also retiring state president of the National League of American Pen Woman for Tennessee.
McLaurin Smith-Williams, Memphis, Tennessee, teaches physics at Christian Brothers High School in Memphis. His hobbies include photography.
Russell H. Strauss, Memphis, Tennessee, is President of the Poetry Society of Tennessee, and wins numerous awards.
Clovita Rice, Little Rock, was editor of *Voices International* and Director of the Arkansas Writers' Conference for many years. She is working of a collection of poetry and prose.
Brett Taylor, Lancing, Tennessee, appears for the first time in Grandmother Earth.
Dr. Malra Treece is Professor Emeritus, College of Business and Economics, University of Memphis. She is author of thirteen college textbooks and has just published the seventh edition of *Successful Communication in Business and the Profession.*.
Florine Petkoff Walters, Helena, Arkansas, has been a member of Poets' Roundtable of Arkansas since 1970, a member of East Central Branch of Poets Roundtable for as long and an associate member of Poetry Society of Tennessee since 1979.
Christine Watt was born in the north-east of England in 1950, graduated from London University with a B.A. Honours degree in history, and emigrated to California in 1973, where she pursued a career in publishing as an editor and writer. My passions are writing, opera (she has been known to sing it!), and rights for animals. She became vegetarian around the age of 7
Alice Heard, Williams, Lynchburg, Virginia is published widely and wins national awards.
Kitty Yeager, Arkadelphia, Arkansas, is a life member of the Poets' Round Table of Arkansas and the Poetry Society of Tennessee. She wins national awards frequently.

Youth Contributors

Angelica DePrimo is a third grade student at Nesconset Elementary School in Nesconset, New York.
Radha Gajjar is a ninth grade student at Houston High School, Germantown, Tennessee
Sarah Gosline is a student in Howell, MI
Carly Kiel is in the 11th grade at White Station High School, Memphis, Tennessee. This is her second appearance in Grandmother Earth.
Carolyn Moir is a 12th grade student at Lexington High School in Lexington, MA
Eric Rogers is a ninth grade student at Memphis University School, in Memphis, Tennessee
Jennifer Leigh Wheeler is a 12th grade student at Santa Fe Christian High School, Solana Beach, California
Rachel White is a sixth grade student at St. Mary's Episcopal School, Memphis, Tennessee

Contributors from Alabama

Jane E. Allen was born in Virginia and, after marriage, moved to Alabama. She was an editor/writer for the Air Force for many years, retiring from Federal service in 1994. She enjoys writing fiction, nonfiction, and poetry--and entering contests. Her works have been included in both national and state publications. Her hobbies are writing, reading, and walking.
Jeanette Barnes is from Madison.
Auguste R. Black, Huntsville, has written several children's books including, *Miracles at the Inn, The Year That Santa Goofed,* and *the Shelby Avenue Gang.*
Betty Cannizzo, Decatur, often wins national awards.
Jack Daniel, a native of Cherokee Alabama, now lives in Memphis, Tennessee. Grandmother Earth has published three of his books.

Reese Danley-Kilgo likes poetry, plants, and people, not necessarily in that order. She reads and writes, gardens and grandmothers, plays Scrabble with friends---in Huntsville, Alabama.

Mary Halliburton has won awards in numerous national contests and is published in a variety of publications through out the U.S. and England. She's an active member of the Alabama State Poetry Society, the Alabama Writers Conclave, Press and Authors, Creative Writers of Montgomery and president of the Montgomery NLAPW Pen Women.

Otis and **Rebecca Henderson** and **Sue Mobley,** live in Madison. Sue was published in *Ordinary and Sacred As Blood: Alabama women speak.*

Susan Murphy has been a humor columnist for the *Over The Mountain Journal* in Birmingham since 1990. Her work has also appeared in the *Birmingham News,* the *Atlanta Journal/ Constitution* and *Atlanta Parent Magazine.* Her book, *Mad Dog Mom,* won the 1998 Small Press Award for Humor. The mother of two college age daughters, Susan is now empty-nesting in Birmingham with her husband, one naughty dog, a neurotic cat, and several nondescript fish.

Esther O' Donald began her writing career early, winning her first essay contest at age 10 and selling her first poetry at age 16. Humorist, essayist and poet, Ms. O' Donald is currently compiling a collection of her verse, as well as completing a play entitled *Crazy Ladies: A Celebration of Aging.* A Seattle poet and writer of the popular *HOW TO COPE* series, whose work has appeared in: *FAMILY CIRCLE, READER'S DIGEST, WRITER'S DIGEST, ARTERIAL TURNS, IPN (INTERNATIONAL POLIO NETWORK)* & other GINI publications and been reprinted and translated worldwide. Former actress, artist, teacher is also wife, mother & grandmother. She was living in Alabama when she entered the contest.

GRANDMOTHER EARTH PUBLICATIONS

Abbott, Barbara, GRANDMOTHER *EARTH'S HEALTHY AND W7SE COOKBOOK,* 1-884289- 13-4 Healthy and easy cooking, but not diet. First layer of fat skimmed from Southern cooking. Optabind binding; $14.

Benedict, Burnette Bolin, *KINSHIP,* 1-884289-08-8 Lyrical poetry set in eastern Tennessee by Knoxville poet. Chapbook, 1995, $6.

Cowden, Frances Brinkley, *VIEW FROM A MISSISSIPPI RIVTR COTTON* SACK-1-884289-03-7, Poetry, family values of farm life in Mississippi County, Arkansas. Cloth, gold imprint, 1993, $15.

TO LOVE A WIALE; 1-884289-06-1. Learning about endangered animals from children and

adults. Children's drawings, poetry and prose, Perfect bound, 1995, $10-00

BUTTERFLIES AND UNICORNS, ED 4, 1-884289-04-5 (Cowden and Hatchett) Poetry for the young and young-at-heart with notes on teaching creative writing. Perfect bound, 1994, $9.00

Daniel, Jack, *SOUTHERN RAILWAY- FROM STEVENSON TO MEMPHIS--1*-884289-17-7 1/2x I I with 400+ photographs, 360 pages, perfect bound, 1996. Signed and numbered upon request. Documents and other papers with heavy emphasis upon history of Southern Railway and its workers, $24.95

MY RECOLLECTIONS OF CHEROKEE, ALABAMA, 1-884289-25-8, 1/2xl 1. 300+ photographs of author's family history and life in early Cherokee, 232 pages, perfect bound, 1998, $22

THOROUGHBREDS OF RAILROADING: YESTERDAY AND TODAY, ISBN 1-884289-26-6 1999, 312 pages, 8 1/2x 11, pictorial history. $29.

Hatchett, Eve Braden, TAKE *TIME TO LAUGH: It's the Music of the Soul.* 1- 884289-00-2, Humorous poetry taking off on Eden theme. Chapbook, limited edition, 1993, $9.

Howard, Elizabeth, *ANEMONES,* 1-884289-27-4, Prize-winning poetry, all previously published, East Tennessee poet, introduction by Connie Green. 1998,$8.95

Schirz, Shirley Rounds, *ASHES TO OAK,* 1-884289-07-X Poetry of the lakes region by widely-published Wisconsin author, chapbook winner, 1995, $6.

SUBSCRIPTION OR DIRECT ORDERS ONLY: $8 per year (otherwise $ 10 each)

1-884289-09-6, GRANDMOTHER EARTH I. 1995
1-884289-14-2, *GRANDMOTHER EARTH II.* 1996
1-884289-16-9, GRANDMOTHER EARTH III. 1997
1-884289-21-5, *GRANDMOTHER EARTH IV-* 1998
1-884289-24-X *GRANDMOTHER EARTH V- 1999*

LIFE PRESS PUBLICATIONS

Boren, Blanche S., *THORNS TO VELVET. Devotionals from a Lifetime of Christian Experience.* 1-884289- 231, Blanche S. Boren, Kivar 7 cloth, 174 pages with 14 photographs. Uplifting look at life's experiences. 1998, $20.

Cowden, Frances Brinkley, *OUR GOLDEN THREAD: Dealing with Grief,* 1-884289-10-x, Ed. Contains personal testimonies and poetry of 40 contributors who deal with different kinds of grief using their personal faith. Kivar 7 cloth, gold imprint, 1996, $15.

ANGELS MESSENGERS OF LOVE AND GRACE, 1-884289-18-5, True stories of angel experiences, 96 pages, perfect bound, 1999, $9.95

Crow, Geraldine Ketchum, *BLOOM WHERE YOU ARE TRANSPLANTED:* Humorous and inspirational approach to moving from the city to the country. 1-884289-12-6 paper, 1996, $10.

Davis, Elaine Nunnally, *MOTHERS OF JESUS.- FROM MATTHEWS GENEALOGY, 1-884289-05-3-* Biblical biography of the five women mentioned in Matthew. 344 pp. Perfect binding, 1994, $12.

EVES FRUIT, 1-884289-11-8--Defense of Eve and implications for the modern woman. Perfect binding, 1995, $10.

Special prices may not apply unless ordered from the publisher. Add $1. 50 postage for one book plus $0.25 each additional book. Mail order to Grandmother Earth and Life Press, P. 0. Box 241986, Memphis, TN 38124.

***

Life Press Writing Association
P. 0. Box 241986
Memphis, TN 38124
(901) 682-6936
grmearth@gateway.net

Members will receive a quarterly newsletter with a poetry lesson or tips on writing in general. Members may submit three poems or one short prose piece each quarter for critique in addition to trying the lesson. The cost is $15 a year. Published writers do critiques. Send SASE with work.

In Memory of Jonathan Bryan Ford
June 13, 1975--January 27, 1999
Grandson of Betty Ford Cowden
Son of Mrs. and Mrs. James Ford
Batesville, Arkansas

In Memory of
December 4, 1916--April 29, 1999
Kenneth D. Thomas
Husband of Edith Thomas,
Memphis, Tennessee

In Honor of
Frances Darby
Whose dedication to poetry is outstanding,.and so is
her hard work for Grandmother Earth publications
Love, A friend and co-worker,
L. A. Smith

Thomas W. McDaniel
Attorney at Law
46 N. Third
Suite 7:30
Memphis, Tennessee 38103
Phone: (901) 525-8612
Fax: (901).527-0450

INDEX

Abbott, 18
Adams, 43
Al-Darahi, 37
Alishan, 44, 46, 66
Allen, 86
Ashworth, 48
Barnes, 88
Beauchamp, 18
Benedict, 37
Black, 96
Brax, 77
Brower, 39, 69
Califf, x, 12
Camp, 29, 40
Cannizzo, 82, 99
Cannon, 6
Carpenter, 49
Cathey, 14
Clemons, 26
Cowden, 70
Crawford, 36
Daniel, 79, 99
Danley-Kilgo, 84
Darby, 68, 101
DePrimo, 72
Dorris, 2
Dyer, 30
Farrar, 8
Foote, 44
Garrison, 32
Gaston, 89
Gajjar, 76
Gosline, 73
Gorrell, 43
Guy, 43
Halliburton, 83
Henderson, O., 87
Henderson, R.,
Hancock, R., 45
Hancock, S., 34
Harrell, 41
Heidelberger, 42
Hepburn, 10
Hinegardner, 51

Hodge, 5, 22
Hoffman, 4
Hogenbirk, v, 7, 42, 88
Howard, 16, 47
Hulsey, 47
Jensen, 42
Jones, J., 17, 90
Jones, P., 63
Kelley, 30
Kiel, 75
Laster, 68, 102
Lee, 53
Levy, 60
Lurrie, 34
McDaniel, 62
McNatt, 19. 21
Marler, 41, 45, 48, 50
Mobley, 78
Moir, 74
Montague, 2, 7, 27
Murphy. A., 57
Murphy, S., 91
O'Donald, 80
Organ, 38
Owens, 12
Penizin, 15
Pfleger, 81
Rakestraw, 52
Rice, 1, 102
Rogers, 72
Schoneman, 44, 66
Stephens, 35
Smith, 46
Smith-Williams, 31
Strauss, 11, 32, 59, 100
Taylor, 31, 44
Treece, 15, 100
Walters, 33
Watt, 54
Wheeler, 77
Williams, 25
White, 71
Yeager, 3

GRANDMOTHER EARTH VI: 2000

Other Grandmother Earth Publications:
Ashes to Oaks
Cherokee Alabama
Grandmother Earth I
Grandmother Earth II
Grandmother Earth III
Grandmother Earth IV
Grandmother Earth V
Grandmother Earth's Healthy and Wise Cookbook
Kinship
Of Butterflies and Unicorns
Take Time to Laugh: It's the Music of the Soul
The Southern Railway: From Stevenson to Memphis
Thoroughbreds of Railroading: Yesterday and Today
To Love a Whale
View from a Mississippi River Cotton Sack

From Life Press:

Angels: Messengers of Love and Grace
Bloom Where You Are Transplanted
Eve's Fruit
The Mothers of Jesus: From Matthew's Genealogy
Our Golden Thread
Thorns to Velvet